Voyages
SKILLS IN EVERYDAY ENGLISH

Stephen Parker
Mike Hayhoe

HEINEMANN
EDUCATIONAL

Heinemann Educational
Halley Court, Jordan Hill, Oxford OX2 8EJ

LONDON EDINBURGH MELBOURNE AUCKLAND
SINGAPORE KUALA LUMPUR NEW DELHI
IBADAN NAIROBI JOHANNESBURG
KINGSTON PORTSMOUTH NH (USA)

Copyright © Stephen Parker and Mike Hayhoe 1989

First published 1989
Reprinted 1990

Printed and bound in Great Britain by
Scotprint Ltd Musselburgh

Design, Phototypeset and Illustrations by Gecko Ltd,
Bicester, Oxon.

Cover Illustration by David Parkins

Hayhoe, Mike
  Voyages: Skills in everday English
  1. English language
  I. Title II. Parker, Stephen
  420

ISBN 0-435-10178-1

ACKNOWLEDGEMENTS

The authors and publishers would like to thank the following for permission to reproduce copyright material:–

John Caldwell   for the extract from *Desperate Voyage* by John Caldwell
Hamish Hamilton Ltd   for the extract from *Highway Home* by Nicholas Fisk
Ocean Youth Club   for the extracts from *Ocean Youth Club Sailing Programme 1986*

It has not been possible in all cases to contact copyright holders. The publishers and author would be pleased to hear from any unacknowledged source and full acknowledgement will be made at the first opportunity.

Please Note: Where you see the symbol ▼ the page or form can be photocopied.

CONTENTS

Voyaging

Chance of a Lifetime	2
Try Your Luck	3
Preparing for the Interview	5
The Interview	6
Making Ready	8
Experts	10
Giving a Talk	11
Ready to Leave?	12
Lifeboat	13
Problems Aboard	16
A Postcard Home	17
Midway	18
Mayday! Mayday!	20
Storm	21
Those Who Hesitate . . .	23
Stranded	25

Island

Survival	28
Sundown Thoughts	29
Shelter	30
Make a Break?	32
Rules	33
Putting It Together	34
Help!	38
Mapping the Island	39
Telling the Tale	41
The Trap	43
Animal Data	44
They've Seen Us!	45
Rescued!	46

Holiday

Action! Holidays!	48
What's on Offer?	49
That Special Holiday	50
Make Their Day	51
Holiday School	52
Planning Forum	54
Two day Holiday	55
Making the Best of It	57
Publicity Brochure	58
Going Public	59
Thank You for Your Enquiry	60
Publicity Launch	62

Scan

Team up with SCAN	64
Finding Out	66
Go for a Logo	67
Headed Paper	68
Making Introductions	69
Sorry, I'll Ask That Again	70
Checklist	71
Asking Questions	72
Sorting Information	73
Choose your Format	74
Sharing SCAN	76

Radio Wideawake

Answering an Advertisement	78
Exploring Radio Programmes	79
What Sort of Programme?	80
Which Part is Yours?	82
Interviewing	83
Getting Going	84
Something to Talk About	86
The Script	87
Filling out the Script	89
Sounds Good	90
Meanwhile . . .	91
The Send Off	92
Going Public	93
Golden Mike Awards	94
And Finally . . .	95

Skills Kits

1 Making notes	96
2 Writing letters	98
3 Advertising	100
4 The interview	101
5 Giving a talk	103
6 Designing a questionnaire	104
7 Reading for information	106
8 The Broadcaster's Training Manual. Part I • Planning a programme	107
9 The Broadcaster's Training Manual. Part II • Recording a programme	109

SKILLS

Skills	Activities	Voyaging 1	2	3	4	5	6	7	8	9	10	11	12	13	14	15	16	Island 1	2	3	4	5	6	7	8	9	10	11	12	13
Note Making				●	●		●							●																●
List Making						●			●	●								●												
Form Filling				●		●																						●	●	
Concise Writing												●	●			●								●	●				●	
Writing Codes																						●								
Drafting Rules																														
Letter Writing		●	●				●																							
Informative Writing			●				●						●							●	●								●	●
Imaginative Writing								●					●	●	●	●			●							●	●		●	
Report Writing													●																	
Media Writing / Presentation																														●
Redrafting														●		●											●			
Group Writing							●																				●			
Illustrating											●	●										●						●	●	
Mapping												●														●			●	
Presentation Skills							●					●												●					●	
Research			●				●	●																						●
Comprehension													●	●											●					●
Analysis													●	●	●															
Decision Making								●	●	●				●	●	●		●			●	●	●							●
Planning							●																							
Organising Information				●		●	●		●																					
Communicating Information								●	●												●			●	●			●	●	
Giving Instructions						●															●		●	●			●			
Persuading						●				●												●	●							
Oral Presentation								●																			●			●
Discussion					●	●			●	●				●	●	●				●	●	●			●	●		●		
Debate																														
Listening						●		●			●																			
Role Play											●																			
Designing Questionnaires																														
Interviewing				●	●																									●

GRID

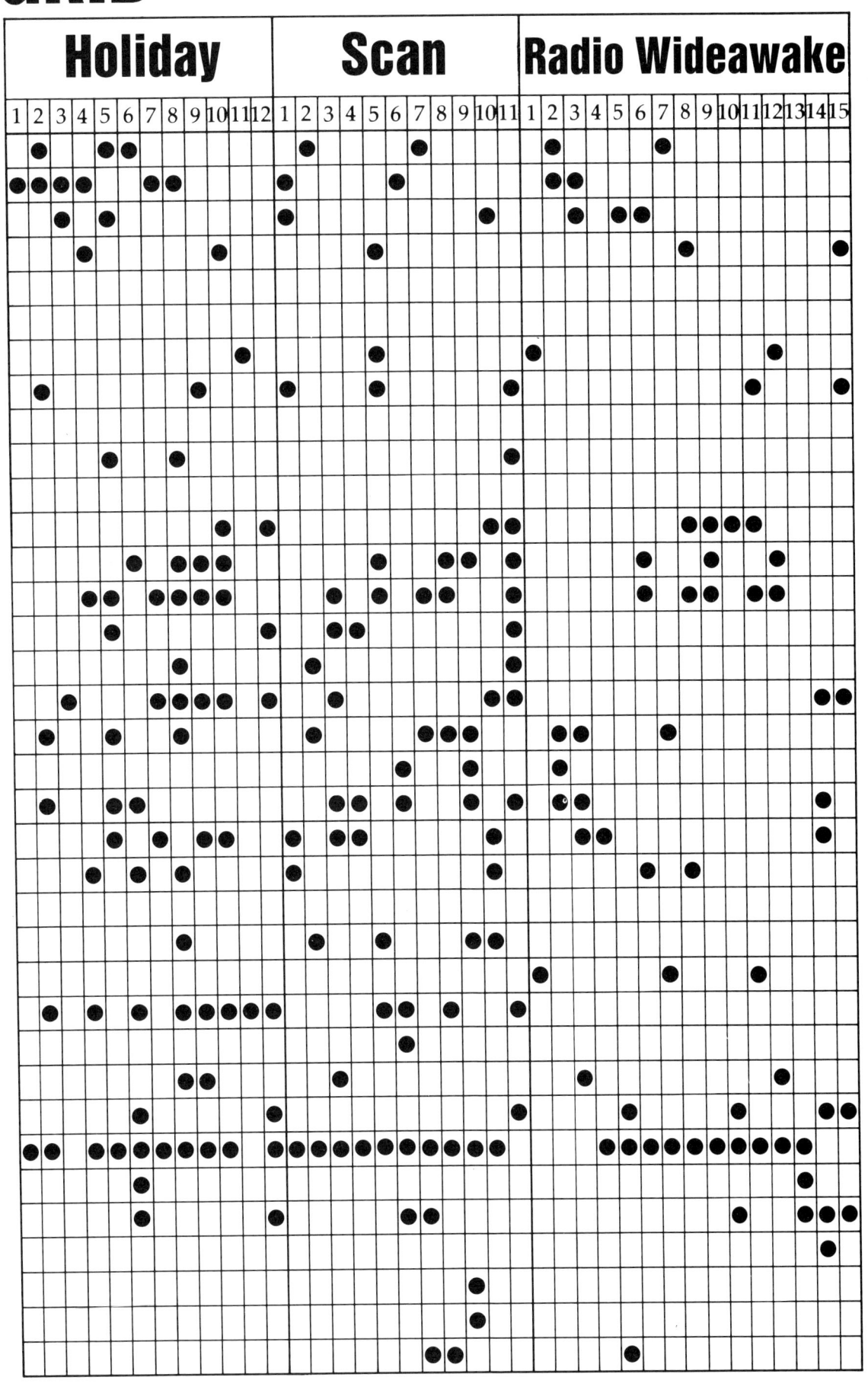

Unit 1
Voyaging

ACTIVITY 1

SKILLS
Letter writing

RESOURCES
Paper

Chance of a Lifetime!

☐ You see this advertisement in a magazine:

Win THE HALF-YEAR OF YOUR LIFETIME!
Win THE PROA COMPETITION!
SAIL THE PACIFIC OCEAN!

A proa is a graceful sailing ship from the East. PROA – Pacific Rim Oceanic Adventures – is an organisation that helps young people to feel the excitement of sailing the mighty Pacific Ocean. This year PROA gives you the chance to sail for six whole months in its own sailing ship the *Nautilus* from Peru to New Zealand.

All you have to do to win your place is apply for the official entry form and details of our PROA competition.

Send to:

PROA
11, Conrad Crescent,
London W1W 9MJ

PROA

1 Write a brief letter to PROA, asking for an entry form.

VOYAGES: SKILLS IN EVERYDAY ENGLISH

ACTIVITY 2

SKILLS
Reading for information, form-filling, writing a formal letter

RESOURCES
Reference books, copy of application form (page 4), paper

Try your luck

☐ These are the forms you receive in answer to your letter. See SKILLS KIT 2, WRITING LETTERS, on page 98 before you begin.

1 Fill in the form and write your letter of application.

Six Questions and Six Answers for the journey of a lifetime!

CHARLES DARWIN was a famous naturalist who made great discoveries during his voyage around the world between 1831 and 1836. He carried out most of his studies in South America and islands in the South Pacific.

Here are the six questions you have to answer on the application form:

1 What was the name of the ship that Darwin sailed in?

2 As he sailed across the Atlantic towards South America, Darwin encountered some islands. They get their name from the Spanish word for "dogs". What are the islands called?

3 Darwin spent a lot of time in the very south of South America, in a part called *Tierra del Fuego*. What does this name mean?

4 One of the ways around the southern tip of South America is through the Straits of Magellan. Why was this route so named?

---

11 Conrad Crescent,
London W1W 9MJ
28/2/92

Dear Competitor,

Thank you for your enquiry about the PROA competition. I enclose details of the competition. You will need to complete the official form, and send a letter of application as well. Good Luck!

Yours sincerely,

Alison Whitby

Competition Organiser

---

5 Darwin's most exciting discoveries were made in the *Galapagos Islands*. Galapagos comes from a Spanish word for a kind of animal which is found on the islands. Which animal is it?

6 Which of these animals would not have been found on an expedition from South America to Australia and New Zealand?
iguana   puma   guanaco
lemur   wallaby   oppossum

VOYAGING 3

PROA COMPETITION APPLICATION FORM

First names .... Surname ....

Date of birth .... Age .... Sex ....

Answers to the competition questions:

| 1 | 2 | 3 |
| 4 | 5 | 6 |

Schools attended   from   to

Best subjects at school

Hobbies and interests

Particular skills useful on the voyage

How much do you know about:

	a lot	a little	nothing
sailing			
navigation			
Morse code			
survival			
botany			
zoology			

Details of someone who can be contacted in an emergency:

Name   Relationship to you

Address

Phone no. (day)   (evening)

2 Include with this form a letter of application. Tell us about yourself, why you want to go on the voyage and why you think you are worth a place.

ACTIVITY 3

SKILLS
Interview skills

RESOURCES
Paper

Preparing for the interview

☐ Now is your chance to prove you are the right person to go on the voyage! You have been invited to an interview where you will be asked by a panel to talk about yourself – your interests, knowledge and skills. Your performance at the interview will be much better if you think beforehand about those three topics and plan what you might say.

1 Make notes on your strengths in:

- your school work
- hobbies and interests
- sport
- personality

See SKILLS KIT 4, THE INTERVIEW, on page 101 for advice.

Your notes should help you prepare for the interview. You will *not* be able to take them in with you.

2 Rule out a form like this and set out your notes in it.

	What I can do	What I want to develop
School		
Hobbies/interests		
Sport		
Personality		

VOYAGING

ACTIVITY 4

The interview

SKILLS

Interviewing, making notes

RESOURCES

Paper, copy of interviewing form (page 7)

☐ PROA has decided to form Interviewing Panels to select people for the Pacific Ocean expedition.

See THE INTERVIEW, SKILLS KIT 4, on page 101. This will help everyone to carry out interviews and complete copies of the Interviewing Form.

1 Form groups of up to four people.
  One of you can be interviewed (the interviewee), and the rest can be the interviewers. An interview should last about 5 minutes.

2 After each interview change over so that one of the interviewers becomes the interviewee. Carry on like this until everyone has been interviewed.

3 One copy of the **Interviewing Form** is to be filled in by one member of the panel of interviewers for each of the interviewees.

4 When all the interviews are over, discuss as a group how well you did as interviewers and interviewees.

PROA INTERVIEWING FORM

Personal details

Name of applicant

Age

Sex

Previous experience: (write down main points)

1 Work of any kind (including Bob-a-Job)

2 Experience with people (including Youth Club)

3 Specialist knowledge (e.g. swimming, sailing)

4 Particular interests (e.g. botany, cooking)

Interview performance

1 Fluency

2 Directness in answering questions

3 Interest in voyage

4 Level of skills

Personal qualities

1 Reliability

2 Sociability

3 How hard working

Overall rating

Recommendation: most suitable job on voyage

ACTIVITY 5

SKILLS
Reading for information, list making, writing instructions for a specific audience

RESOURCES
Example of instructions, paper

Making ready

☐ You receive this letter in the post a few weeks after the interview. Read it carefully and then turn to the next page.

> 11, Conrad Crescent,
> London W1W 9MJ.
> 16/2/92
>
> Dear Expedition Member,
>
> Congratulations! You have been selected to join the crew of the sailing ship Nautilus on its voyage this summer from Peru to New Zealand.
>
> The crew will meet in London on 1st August to learn more about the trip before flying to Peru to join the ship.
>
> You will realise that space on Nautilus is limited. We do not give exact instructions on what to bring with you for a voyage which lasts for half a year, but the enclosed information should be of help to you.
>
> With best wishes for your packing,
>
> Yours sincerely,
>
> *Alison Whitby*
>
> Competition Organiser

☐ Here are the instructions which an organisation called "The Ocean Youth Club" sends to people who are preparing to sail with them *for a week or so* in northern waters. Read them carefully and see how sensible and detailed they are.

What You Must Bring With You

1. CLOTHING

It is always much colder at sea than you expect, so take an extra sweater and another pair of socks, but remember that stowage space is very limited, and there is nowhere suitable to hang jackets and dresses.

Minimum recommended kit for a week
TWO COMPLETE CHANGES OF WARM CLOTHING.
THESE ARE THE CLOTHES YOU WILL SAIL IN.
Trousers and sweaters should be warm and tough. Jeans are O.K. Shirts should tuck well into your trousers.
TWO WARM SWEATERS which should cover your hips when stretching or bending over.
SOFT SHOES — gym or track shoes with a non-skid sole, or a pair of cheap canvas sailing shoes. Flip flops and hard soled shoes are dangerous, and you will not be allowed to wear them onboard.
SOCKS — at least two pairs of thick wool socks or football socks.
SLEEPING BAG — ESSENTIAL — if you haven't got one, try to borrow one from your school, youth group or friends — but don't come without one!
TOWEL AND WASHING GEAR — Obvious but sometimes forgotten. Include sun tan lotion for sun and windburn and grease for dry lips.
TORCH — Useful below decks as it saves putting on the main lights and disturbing those asleep.
TEA TOWEL — Sixteen people use a lot of crockery and cutlery!
OLD TOWEL FOR NECKCLOTH — Stops the drips running down your neck.
TIDY CLOTHING SUITABLE FOR SHORE WEAR — This would be what you travel in.
SWIMMING COSTUME
WELLINGTON BOOTS — Must have non-slip soles.
HATS — a woolly hat at least, and a sun hat if you are worried about sunburn.
GLOVES — Woollen gloves are fine and easily dried.
DON'T FORGET — Vests or T shirts, Pyjamas, Hankies and changes of underwear.
PLEASE STOW ALL YOUR KIT IN SOFT, SQUASHY BAGS, FRAMELESS RUCKSACKS or similar. SUITCASES AND RUCKSACK FRAMES CANNOT BE STOWED ONBOARD.

You are recommended to pack all your clothes and your sleeping bag into plastic bags inside your kitbag to stop them getting wet when you go onboard.

2. PASSPORTS
Passports are required **for any cruise except two day week-ends and three day cruises** on most vessels - check each boat's sailing programme for details of passport requirement. Visitors' passports are sufficient.

3. PERSONAL EFFECTS
Do bring your camera, binoculars etc., if you wish, but remember that the Club cannot accept any liability for loss or damage.
Please do not bring **transistor radios or tape recorders** as they can interfere with navigation equipment.

4. POCKET MONEY
This is entirely up to you, but between £15-£30 is probably enough. Bring sterling and change your money abroad if necessary.

5. FISHING TACKLE
There will be opportunities to fish from the boats, but fishing rods are not necessary as hand-lines are quite sufficient. If you bring your fishing tackle, please ensure that you don't leave hooks and lines lying around, and that you check with the skipper before you start fishing.

6. DOCTOR'S CERTIFICATE
Check the section on the reverse of the *Booking Form*. If you have a medical condition or disability, you must send your *Doctor's Certificate* to the Bookings Office when you book your cruise - and ensure that you have an adequate supply of drugs etc. when you join your cruise.

7. SUNDRIES
Sweets, chocolate, a paperback or two and spare film for your camera are worth tucking in a corner of your bag.

8. MUSICAL INSTRUMENTS
If you can play the mouth organ, tin whistle or guitar - or any other easily stowed musical instrument - bring it along.

What Ocean Youth Club Provides
Each vessel carries
Lifejackets - Oilskin Jackets and Trousers - Safety Harnesses
for every member of the crew. The food is good and plentiful and is cooked by the crew members.
R.Y.A. Logbooks are sold onboard, and members are encouraged to take part in this excellent training scheme.

☐ You will be sailing for *six months*. Your locker space is only one cubic metre – roughly the volume of a tea-chest. You may meet some cool weather and cold seas, but much of your travelling will be in warmer climates.

1 Read the "The Ocean Youth Club" list carefully and think about the additional information PROA have given you.

2 Produce a list of what you propose to take. Remember that you have not much room.

3 Compare your list with someone else's.

4 Work with a partner to write packing instructions for members of the PROA Expedition. Try to imitate the clear, friendly, but firm, style of the **What You Must Bring With You** sheet. You can use the same basic headings if you want to, but feel free to experiment. You might produce your instructions as a pamphlet, or as a small poster. You might use diagrams or sketches, or even cartoons. Decide on the best way to make sure that people *will read* what you have written and *will do* what you suggest.

ACTIVITY 6

Experts

SKILLS
Researching for a talk

RESOURCES
Library, paper resources

☐ Experts will be needed to lead others in the work of the expedition. The following roles are likely to be the most important:

Botanists: **a)** gather information about plants on the islands visited
b) identify plants
c) look after living plants and preserve specimens.

Cooks: **a)** know about healthy diets
b) know how to cook in cramped conditions with limited resources
c) know about foods available across the Pacific region.

Crew Members: **a)** know about sailing and sailing ships
b) advise on swimming for survival
c) know types of knots and their uses.

Navigators: **a)** know about the Pacific from Peru to Australia/New Zealand
b) understand nautical instruments.

Safety Officers: **a)** know how to use safety equipment including life-boats
b) are able to instruct the crew on what to do in an emergency
c) advise on land survival in the event of shipwreck.

Zoologists: **a)** gather information about animal life (fish/birds/reptiles/mammals) likely to be found on the voyage
b) advise on food resources
c) advise on sources of danger.

1 Choose one role which interests you, and find out as much as you can about the subject. (See SKILLS KIT 7, READING FOR INFORMATION on page 106 for advice.)

2 Visit the library to start finding information. An encyclopaedia might be helpful in the first place, but you may need then to look for books in the specialist section of the library.

3 Ask people who might know something about your subject for their help.

4 Make notes on your findings and keep these carefully for later.

ACTIVITY 7

SKILLS
Oral presentation skills

RESOURCES
Prepared notes from Activity 6 (page 10)

Giving a talk

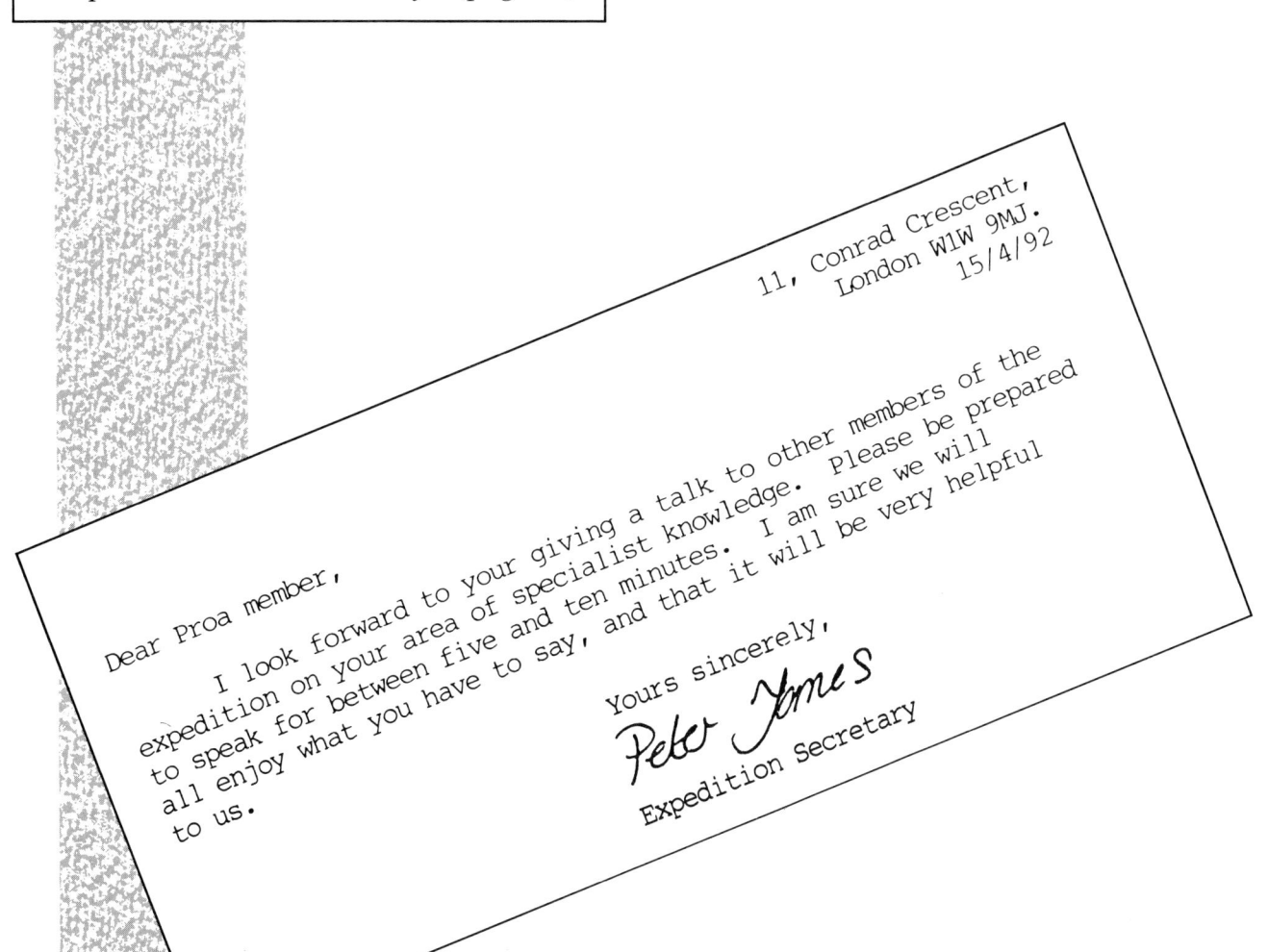

> 11, Conrad Crescent,
> London W1W 9MJ.
> 15/4/92
>
> Dear Proa member,
>
> I look forward to your giving a talk to other members of the expedition on your area of specialist knowledge. Please be prepared to speak for between five and ten minutes. I am sure we will all enjoy what you have to say, and that it will be very helpful to us.
>
> Yours sincerely,
> Peter Jones
> Expedition Secretary

1. Prepare your talk on the expert role you have researched. See SKILLS KIT 5, GIVING A TALK on page 103 for help and advice.
2. Give a talk of about three minutes.

ACTIVITY 8

SKILLS
Decision making, listing, free writing

RESOURCES
Paper

Ready to leave?

☐ What arrangements do you need to make before you leave on the expedition? Think of all the activities you normally do, all the people you know, all the groups that you belong to.

What do you need to cancel? Whom do you need to inform? You might need to cancel a regular magazine delivery. You might have to tell friends, or a club leader that you will be away for six months. There may be pets which someone else must look after.

1 Begin by making a list of all the things that you need to arrange.

2 Choose one of these and write a letter explaining the situation, and advising on anything which the person may need to do for you while you are away.

Now that you have told everyone that you are leaving, you are on your own with your thoughts until the expedition leaves. Although you will be looking forward to your adventure, it has not yet begun. What do you think you will miss? People? Places? Activities? Six months is going to be a long time away.

3 Make a list of what you will miss and shape it into a poem or a diary entry.

ACTIVITY 9

Lifeboat

SKILLS
Listing priorities, informal debate

RESOURCES
Diagram of boat, photocopy of competition sheet (pages 14 and 15)

In the first week of the expedition all new members are given this handout and copies of the next two pages.

All the lifeboats and liferafts on the *Nautilus* are of the latest design and contain official safety and survival equipment.

To help pass the time on the early part of the voyage, we are holding a competition. Imagine that you have to rely on an ordinary rowing boat instead of a lifeboat. You and your team have to decide what you would put in it and where you would stow these items on board. You will need enough gear to survive for fourteen days.

1 Each of you should *make a list* of the ten most important items to include on the boat. Give each item a star rating, with five stars for the most important items, down to a single star for the least important.

2 Now *compare your lists*. See where you agree and disagree about items and about their star ratings. Then produce an *agreed list* of items, again with the most important items having a high star rating.

3 Make sure you have a copy of the plan of 'your' boat. As a team, decide what should be stowed where. *Mark where each item is to go in the boat.* Remember: you do not have much space; you do not want a top-heavy boat; you will need certain items close to hand while you are at sea and others might be needed only if you get to land. You may not be able to include all the items you want.

4 *Produce an agreed list* of the items that you have stowed. In the left hand column, name each item and how many or how much you propose to load. In the right hand column, give your reason for choosing each item. Make this report as formal and as clear as you can.

The competition will be judged by everyone taking part. One team wins for producing the most sensible loading plan. One team wins for having the most sensible loading list. The team which wins both competitions will be a super team indeed!

1 In your team, produce the marked diagram and list for the competition.

VOYAGING 13

THE LIFEBOAT COMPETITION

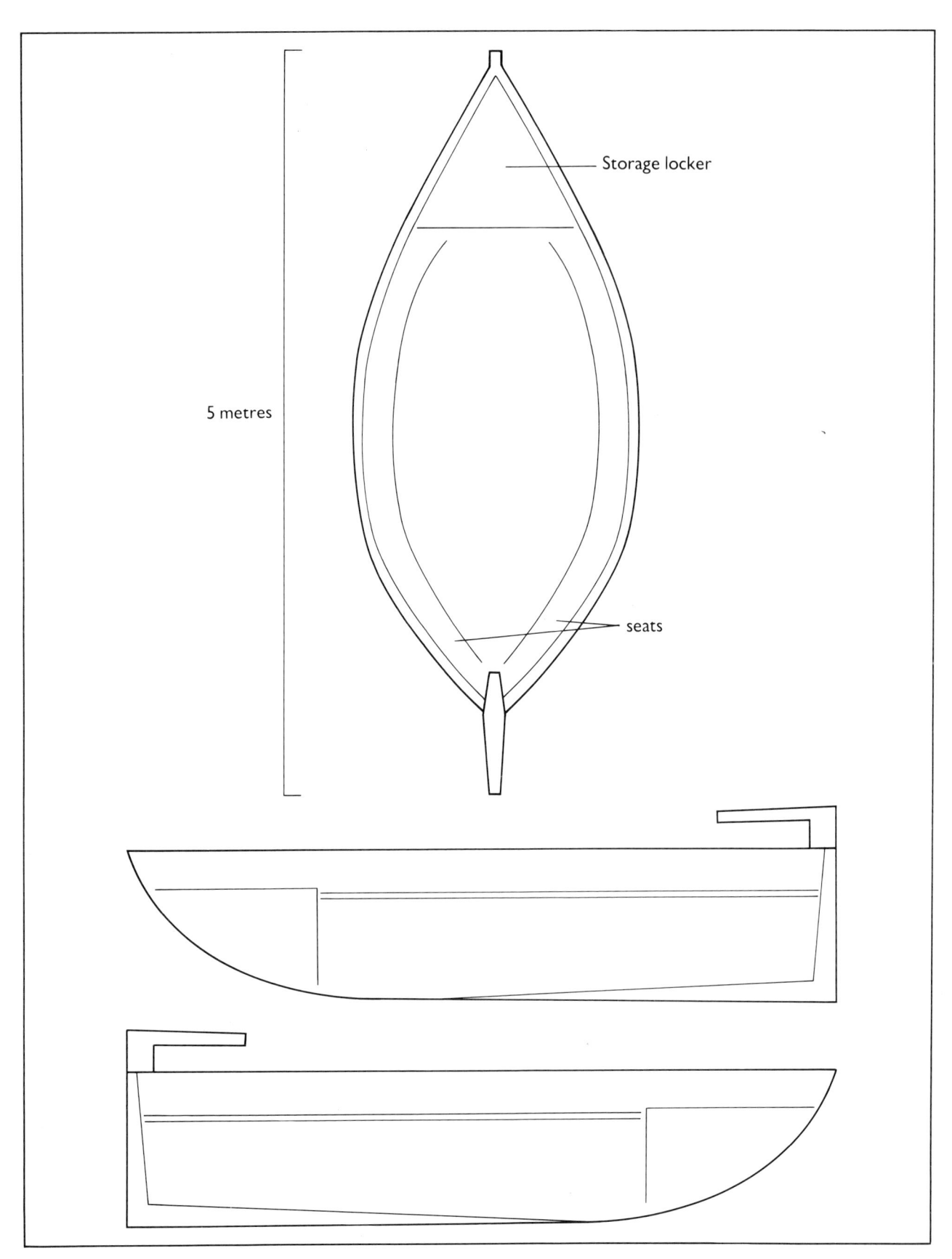

5 metres

Storage locker

seats

THE LIFEBOAT COMPETITION

Item	Quantity	Reasons

ACTIVITY 10

SKILLS
Role playing

RESOURCES
Drama area

Problems aboard

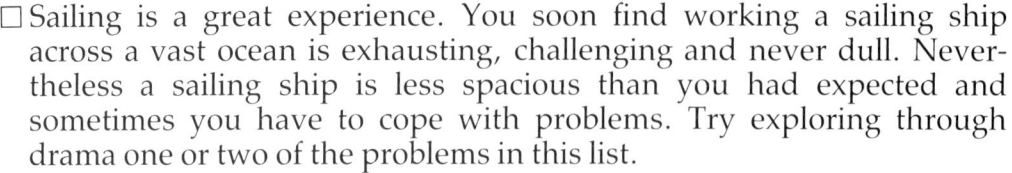

☐ Sailing is a great experience. You soon find working a sailing ship across a vast ocean is exhausting, challenging and never dull. Nevertheless a sailing ship is less spacious than you had expected and sometimes you have to cope with problems. Try exploring through drama one or two of the problems in this list.

1 You are not happy about the food you have been getting recently. The cooks claim that they are doing their best and that there are reasons why the food is not as good as it was. Hold a discussion with them about the situation.

2 In your cabin there are four bunks. Two people keep leaving their things scattered over the bunks and floor, whilst two want the whole cabin, which is very small, to be kept tidy. Talk about your problem.

3 Something goes missing and theft is suspected. It may be that there is a thief or it may be that the lost item has just been misplaced. Either act out how you lay a trap to catch a thief, *or* hold a group meeting about the problem.

4 Some sounds can be very annoying in confined quarters over a long period. One of the crew whistles constantly, without realising it; another plays a musical instrument (badly) when others do not want to listen; and one person snores, disturbing the sleep of others.

5 You find out that someone has been smoking in one of the storage lockers below decks. This could be very dangerous because of the fire risk, apart from the risk to that person's health.

6 The ship must keep going 24 hours a day, and at night the safety of all depends on a good watch being kept not just by the crew member steering the ship but by a lookout in the bows. If a lookout was found to be asleep, what action would you take?

7 A ship's crew must have officers who take responsibility for the running of the ship, which means giving orders. If one of the officers seems to be too harsh, shouting at the crew and being rude, what could you do?

8 On board the ship you have no television and no radio, and have to make your own entertainment. Could you put together a variety show, with songs, sketches, readings and so on, to entertain yourselves one evening at sea?

VOYAGES: SKILLS IN EVERYDAY ENGLISH

ACTIVITY 11

A postcard home

SKILLS

Concise writing

RESOURCES

Postcard-sized card, examples of picture postcards (optional)

☐ A postcard gives you very little space in which to write your message, but it can mean a lot to the person receiving it. It is such a pity to write only "Having a nice time. Wish you were here", giving nothing of the feel of the place and your reactions to it.

1 Read this message, and then write your own postcard to someone at home who would like to hear from you. Use sixty words or fewer.

> Dear Paul,
> Our first coral island! Sailed into a lagoon at dawn with sun rising over palm trees. Anchored in a sandy bay — sea brilliant blue, so clear you can see fish on bottom. Taking on water and fresh fruit — ever eaten mango? Voyage going well — making good friends.
> Best Wishes, Heather

> Paul Kenyon,
> 43 Lansdown Rd,
> Brentfield,
> Essex BR4 2KW
> England

VOYAGING 17

ACTIVITY 12

Midway

SKILLS
Report writing

RESOURCES
Paper

☐ You are now half-way through your journey and are resting for a few days on an island. You have time to write a report for PROA magazine on how the expedition is going. PROA Magazine is for past members, parents, friends and sponsors who want to read lively accounts of expeditions.

Parents and sponsors are likely to want to know that your voyage is safe and useful. Past members and friends might also enjoy hearing about your hardships, but in a lively way without too much doom and gloom.

Here are two examples taken from the Ocean Youth Club's magazine. In the first extract, you can see how the writer has created a cheerful and amusing account which is ideal for a magazine. In the second the writer has used very few words and lots of sketches to give a report.

I awoke next morning to find us close to Cape Finisterre and the rugged coastline of Spain on *Lipton's* port beam. What a terrific day's sailing that was, ending in a beautiful evening sunset as *Lipton* slipped gently into the natural harbour of Vigo...

Shopping for food proved an eye-opener. The price of fresh meat was astronomical, but this was countered by keen bargaining for a cheap crate of tangerines. After a lively night we were on our way again...

Gales were next on the agenda and we had a hair-raising 36 hours. The wind increased to force 7, blowing force 8 squalls occasionally and building up mountainous seas behind us. *Lipton* surfed along the crests in an alarming manner before sinking into the deep troughs. The waves looked enormous, reminding me of an alpine range with their white tops; the only difference being that they were all on the move and regularly showered us with an avalanche of water...

With the yawing motion, cooking below was quite a trial. Pans leapt around the gimballed stove and out of the oven when the door was opened. Polly produced an incredible apple crumble which somersaulted twice before landing on the pan of pork chops which preceded it out of the oven. The chops tasted delicious, though the apple crumble had a distinct choppy flavour. That night waves drowned the cockpit twice, pouring down below in spite of the hatch covers...

---

18 VOYAGES: SKILLS IN EVERYDAY ENGLISH

A Week In August

We joined Theodora *at Brightlingsea.*

There were 10 Sea Rangers from East Ilford (all very beautiful)

two handsome mates

and the skipper with his personal mate.

We sailed on Sunday night for Rotterdam. It was quite rough.

We arrived at Rotterdam on Monday and sailed up the new waterway to the yacht harbour.

Next day we sailed under the bridge and tied up alongside a barge about half-way to Dordrecht.

On Wednesday we explored Dordrecht and then tacked all the way down to Veere where we lay in the new yacht marina. There were lots of barges to dodge on the way.

The tides were strong and the weather squally.

Veere is very picturesque but not so much as it used to be. It has a quaint clock tower and very attractive ice creams.

Through the canal to Flushing where the ship was given a good clean up and a dose of paint. The crew walked about 50 miles for a good square meal (NOT PILCHARDS) before braving the dreaded rigours of the homeward voyage.

But indeed we got a sudden blow when near home.

There was not much fair tide left so we upped helm and ran into Harwich where we left the ship after a first rate week.

1 Write a lively report of *your* journey so far.

ACTIVITY 13

SKILLS
Free writing

RESOURCES
Paper

Mayday! Mayday!

☐ The time has come to sail on. Here are some impressions of what happens next.

1 Write them up in any way you see fit – a letter home, a personal diary, an album of sketches.

Mayday! Mayday! Fishing boat RORATOA calling! Giant waves swamping us! Position...

ACTIVITY 14

SKILLS
Group writing

RESOURCES
Story extract, paper

Storm!

☐ In Nicholas Fisk's exciting adventure story *High Way Home* three teenagers and an expert sailor take a sailing boat across a tropical sea when a storm strikes and brings them catastrophe.

1. Read the extract on the next page. Discuss with others how Nicholas Fisk has made it exciting.
   - What has he done to grab and keep hold of your attention?
   - How has he described the storm?
   - How does he have each character behave?
   - How does he use your senses – of colour, of movement, of sound, of temperature, of pressure?
   - Try to compare which bits you like best.

2. Work out as a team the sequence for *your* storm disaster. Split it up into as many sections as there are people in your team. Each of you adopts a section and is responsible for writing it in rough draft.

3. Come together as an editorial team and work to improve each section. When you are satisfied with what you have developed as a team, take your original section and write it up neatly.

4. Now assemble all the sections into a booklet, so that all your contributions come together as a complete account of your storm.

VOYAGING 21

'Rope everything down! Secure! Harness on!' yelled Torry and flung pieces of rope at him. He began fumbling with the body harness. He could catch glimpses of Barry doing the same thing and imitated him. The harness went round chest and shoulders. Then he ran to the mizzen mast and helped drag the sail down and make it fast.

On the horizon, the black wall was still blacker, still nearer. A hot puff of wind tugged the canvas in his hands. A single puff, nothing more. Then dead calm again. . .

Rupert looked around for something else to do. Baba was lashing down hatches. He helped, trying to copy the knots her nimble brown hands made. She yelled 'No, no!' and he thought she was angry with him again. But she only wanted him to go round all the doors and hatches and ports – 'If there's a bolt or a catch or anything else, *fasten* it! Lock *everything* up!'

He ran through the boat, panting and worried, looking for things to fasten. It suddenly occurred to him that they were making an almighty fuss about nothing and slowed down. He had heard, vaguely, of 'tropical revolving storms'; surely they took hours to build up and strike? But then Torry was framed in the cabin door, shouting 'Air bottle! Seen the air bottle? Where?'

Rupert had seen it. He got it. Torry shouted 'OK, OK, the inflatable! Blow her up!' and ran away again. Rupert said 'Where –?' and had to go and ask Baba. She pulled a face, dragged him behind her like a naughty child to the cabin roof where the inflatable dinghy lived. . . He pulled the tag on the cylinder and the bright yellow inflatable went 'Phhhh!' and swelled, much too fast. She shouted 'Chuck it overboard! Overboard!' so he did. If Baba had not grabbed the line attached to it it would have floated away . . . He felt himself go scarlet with shame and anger. The inflatable bobbed on the water, jaunty and jolly, mocking him.

'You! You! You! Over here! Double! Torry bellowed. The three of them lined up in front of him. Torry grabbed the cable from Rupert's harness and operated the spring shackle. 'Clip it like this, see? To the guard rails. Snap it on to anything solid.' The black wall was advancing. The surface of the sea suddenly turned from blue to slate grey as the wind whipped it. They felt warm spray.

'Mayday?' * said Barry.

Torry was still for a moment, thinking. He made up his mind. 'We haven't been hurt yet,' he said. 'So it's no good yelling. It might be hours, a day. It might miss us by a hundred miles . . . No, we must face things alone. . .'

The sky darkened suddenly. More warm spray. The sky was turning leaden. The black wall was rushing on yet there was still no real wind, just the hot, tearing gusts over the water. First a gust making a thin whine through the standing rig: then nothing, a dull silence. . .

Then it hit. Rupert had expected to have to wait until the black wall itself reached them – but it came out of nothing, out of thick air. It slammed *Moana* like a huge punch. She reeled and staggered. Stays shrieked, the main mast groaned in its footings, something crashed in the cabin ('My fault!' thought Rupert) and Barry was sprawled on the deck, his harness pulled to a peak over his chest. Then the wind changed from punching to blasting. It came over them like a huge hand sweeping over a chessboard. It seemed to pick up *Moana* and throw her. She felt as if she were airborne, riding backwards in the thundering, screaming blast of air, high above the sea. Torry was struggling with the tiller, the big muscles of his arms standing out. He arched his back and kicked the throttle wide open with a bare foot. To keep her into the wind, thought Rupert. But *Moana* felt too small, she was nothing in this huge sea, this almighty wind . . .

Barry was shouting and pointing. Torry saw him – he could not hear him – and yelled, 'Yes! Safer there!' Barry clawed his way to the cabin door, fumbled with ropes and locks, braced himself to hold it secure. The half door opened – and seemed to explode in his face and fly away in splinters over the dark sea. Barry sank to his knees, face twisted with pain, holding his hands under his armpits. After a while, he freed his hands and inspected them. One was bleeding but he could move all his fingers. He clambered doggedly into the cabin on hands and knees.

It was cold. The raindrops hit like blunted bullets. Rupert could hardly see Baba. She was bracing herself, methodically, against the cabin and the rail. Her black hair flew straight across her forehead in glistening streaks. The tail of her sweater was fluttering furiously over a patch of wet brown skin. Her lower lip stuck out with concentration. She's all right, thought Rupert. Thank God. And Barry was sending out Mayday on the radio.

---

* Mayday is a distress signal, like SOS in Morse Code.

ACTIVITY 15

SKILLS
Group decision making

RESOURCES
Watch, photocopy of Decision Sheet (page 24)

Those who hesitate...

Here is a test of your ability to make decisions under pressure. **Before you read any further,** join a group, have ready a pen, a watch and a copy of the **Decision Sheet**.

What has happened
In a violent squall, in blinding rain and spray from huge waves, the *Nautilus* has struck a rock and is sinking fast. You were thrown heavily against a bulkhead by the collision. You are dazed by the shock, but not hurt.
Through the spray you can see an island in the distance, probably beyond the reef which you have struck. With luck you may get ashore, but there is no knowing whether it is inhabited. You may land with nothing to help you survive.

> YOU MUST DECIDE TWO THINGS:
> 1 What to take with you.
> 2 How to get ashore.

Go below! The captain says that you and your group have only *five minutes* to collect any equipment which will help you to survive. You know what you packed to come on board ship.
Look back at your list. In the left-hand column of the **Decision Sheet**, make a list of items you decide to take – from nought to nine. Start your watch NOW. Stop choosing when five minutes are up.

* * * *

Now you have with you what you need to survive shipwreck on an island. Back on deck in the swirling wreckage you can see:
- a five metre spar with a tangle of light rope around it
- a large plastic barrel with two handles on the side
- a lifeboat jammed under a fallen mast
- a heavy black tarpaulin

You can jump straight away OR you can take one of these to help with your survival. You have *two minutes* to decide.
On the **Decision Sheet** tick the appropriate box for what you decide. Start your watch NOW.

Time's up!

The *Nautilus* slips slowly into the deep water on the ocean side of the reef as huge waves crash right over her main deck. If you have not agreed on a way of getting off, you go down with her.

You now have time to think over whether you did the right thing. Look at the **Decision Sheet** and fill in the reasons for your decisions.

Tell the other groups what you decided and compare your decisions with theirs. Who has the best chance of surviving the storm and surviving on a desert island?

DECISION SHEET

Below deck

List what you decide to take. (Add reasons why *later*)

	Item	Reason Why
1		
2		
3		
4		
5		
6		
7		
8		
9		

On deck

Tick what you choose to do. (Add reasons for and against *later*.)

Action	Choice	Reasons For	Reasons Against
Jump straight away			
Take spar and tangled rope			
Take barrel			
Take lifeboat			
Take tarpaulin			

ACTIVITY 16

Stranded

SKILLS
Comprehension, descriptive writing

RESOURCES
Text provided, paper

☐ A tropical island can be beautiful, if you have chosen to be there for a holiday – but it can be very hostile if your boat is being battered by a storm upon its jagged reefs.
Look at this true account as one sailor's storm-smashed boat nears such an island.

1. Read it (or hear it) at least twice.
2. Jot down five bits of it – words or phrases or longer bits – that you find particularly good.
3. Write alongside each of the five; **a** which of your senses it appeals to, and; **b** which of your emotions. You will need these brief notes later.

> **Pagan** caught the swell of a roller, rode in on its back, and crashed stem-to against the coral wall. She shivered as though struck by shell fire. I was sitting near the port rail. One of her planks sprung, pointing away from the stern. I could see the water gush through it. In a moment she settled by the bow, the deck was awash, the fore scuttle covered. In no time I was sitting to my pockets in water. I could only sit and watch – the decks were too lurching to permit me to stand.
> I could hear a horrible noise as **Pagan** pounded against the reef at the beam. Only the watertight stern section was buoyant. The bow was still going down. Water was up to my waist. The next two rollers lifted the stern on the reef......... I slipped down the abrupt incline and fell free of the boat onto the coral, only to be overwhelmed by a sea that twisted me into a somersault and threw me back on to the shallower coral ground. I gathered myself up, shook free of the grasping water, and somehow moved a few feet to where it was safe.
> I had backed away from my battered boat onto the dry coral and sat cursing the bullying sea. **Pagan** was thrown up onto where the water was knee deep. Each time a roller broke over her she shuddered and ground her planks on the sharp coral.
> Behind me the jagged reef ran for two hundred yards. I turned and staggered in the stiff-legged way of the gaunt and hungry to the brink of the reef. There the lagoon dropped to a depth of nine fathoms, where a garden land of coral formations grew. Tiny fish were as visible in fifty feet of water as in fifty of clear air. I shunned the water like poison, knowing that if I should fall in, I would sink like a weight...
> I waded to the sloping deck and climbed uncertainly aboard, looking for something on which to float across the deep lagoon. **Pagan** was on her

beam, teetering either way, likely to lob over again. Knife in hand I hacked away the stout lashings holding the thirty-five foot mast to the deck. I jumped off and sloshed to where the water was knee-deep, and looked back. The rising sea was whamming **Pagan** *and threatening to bowl her over. Suddenly* **Pagan** *jammed her beam into the coral and clumped over from her beam onto her decks. The hull, pointing skyward, was ghastly with barnacles and scars and loose planking.*

I felt drowsy but there was no place to lie down. The growing waves were pushing me back away from the boat. Then the mast worked loose and I took hold of it. I held to it as the sea drove it slowly across the lagoon, I climbed on its heaviest part, straddling it, floating on it.

My arms and legs were dangling in the water, my head and chest resting on the hard curved surface. For a long time I lay watching the island as I floated off on to the lagoon. Finally I drifted off to a sleeplike drowse. I awakened when the mast scraped on the soft shore. I was in a small alcove fronted with bright sand, overtowered by a beetling wall of volcanic rock. I plodded out of the water on to the white sand. I slumped into the inviting warmth and fell asleep.

John Caldwell: *Desperate Voyage*

The sailor who wrote about that landing was on his own. Luckily, you were not.

4 Work with your fellow-survivors and write together a very brief, very 'flat' account of your own sea drama. It might read something like this:

> Midday – hazy sun – boat in dead calm – crew uneasy – heavy atmosphere – total quiet
>
> 2.00pm – Dark cloud low on horizon – slight breeze – very hot – first waves
>
> 2.30pm – Great wave – ship's masts broken – ship carried helplessly towards land

5 Now bring your 'flat' version to life – or part of it. Work with a partner to recreate the excitement, confusion and horror of your powerlessness as you were cast upon the island. Catch the merciless energy of the forces that made you helpless. Create for your readers what you did to try to survive in the last moments of your boat's existence. Share with them how you felt.

VOYAGES: SKILLS IN EVERYDAY ENGLISH

Unit 2
Island

ACTIVITY 1

SKILLS
Decision making

RESOURCES
Paper

Survival

☐ You have been shipwrecked on what seems to be a deserted island in the tropics. The storm which smashed your ship is over. You have survived – but only just. You have no idea where you are. All you know is that you are on an empty beach which slopes steeply to the sea. Even now, the sea shows its temper as waves smash on the wet sand. There is no other movement, no other sound.

At least your disaster has left you unharmed. You ache and have some bruises and small cuts, but no wounds, no broken bones. That is something to be grateful for. The storm has dealt less kindly with your clothing and the gear you had on the ship. You remain dressed decently, but pockets and baggage have been badly damaged. In fact, they contain few of the items you usually carry. In any case, you will need to travel light, if you are to escape from this trap of a beach.

1 Check what you actually have with you at *this* moment. You can keep *only three items*. Choose things which might help you survive on this unknown island.
2 You must also use your skills in your struggle for survival. Decide which *three skills* are going to be the most important.
3 Now make a list like this:

ITEMS	POTENTIAL USES
1	
2	
3	
SKILLS	WHY YOU WILL NEED THEM
1	
2	
3	

4 Share your lists of items and skills with a partner. Compare what you have chosen. Decide upon the three most important items from your two lists and the three most important skills. Be prepared to defend your choices to other groups or to the whole class.

ACTIVITY 2

SKILLS
Descriptive writing

RESOURCES
Paper

Sundown thoughts

☐ You look around. Behind you, steep cliffs block the view. They look at least fifteen metres high. They curve round to either side of you and jut out into the hostile sea. The beach provides temporary safety, but that may be all. It is time to start thinking about survival.

The air is cooling and a slight breeze is coming from off the sea. It feels pleasant at first, but then it starts to chill. The sun is going down fast towards the horizon. You can feel the darkness rising around you.

A lot has happened to you today.

1 Write down your thoughts and feelings as you prepare to spend your first night on the empty beach of this deserted island.

ACTIVITY 3

Shelter

SKILLS

Decision making, writing and illustrating instructions

RESOURCES

Paper

☐ Your first priority after the shipwreck is water, but that soon arrives. The late afternoon brings rain. It floods down from the clouds lumbering in from the sea until you feel that you could drown under its attack. But the water is warm, it drenches the salt off you and you drink with your cupped hands.

The violent gift stops as quickly as it began. Now your priority is shelter – somewhere to give you a chance to be safe and dry and warm – somewhere to sleep.

What can you do to make a shelter? You walk along the shoreline, where the sea meets the land. You walk along the high-tide line and are glad to see that it does not reach to the cliffs.

You see the items on the next page on the beach.

You would like to use almost all of them to build your shelter, but your good sense tells you to keep some of them . . . for who knows what you will need later?

1. You decide to use eight of the objects for your shelter. Choose them.

2. Draw a rough sketch of your shelter. Underneath it, jot down brief notes on its construction.

3. Produce neat, clear illustrations and a carefully written list of instructions on how to build a shelter for an official book or wall chart on how to survive.

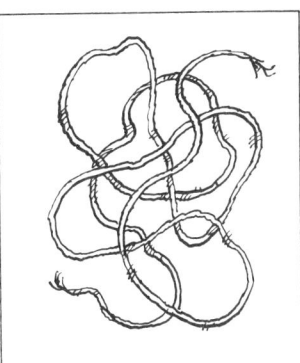

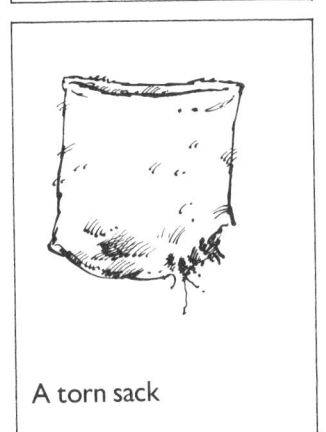

Two metres of strong nylon cord	An empty bean tin	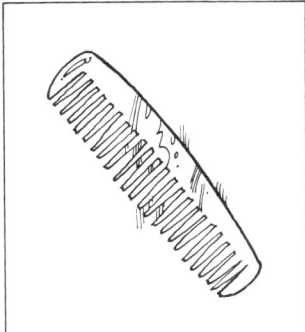 A comb made of aluminium	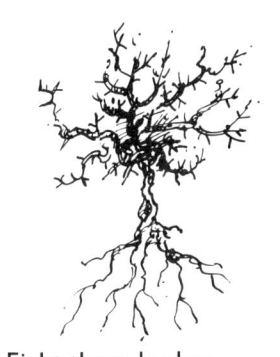 Eight thorn bushes with deep roots
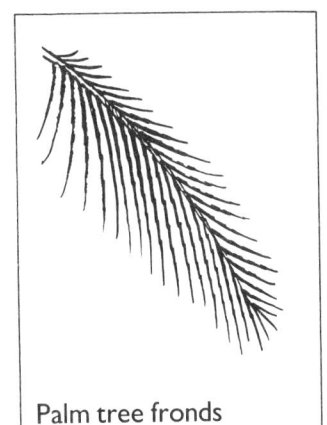 Palm tree fronds	 An empty bottle	Ten three-inch nails	Five large flints
A torn sack	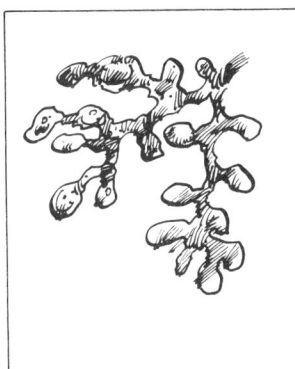 Dried seaweed at the high tide mark	 Three metres of heavy rope	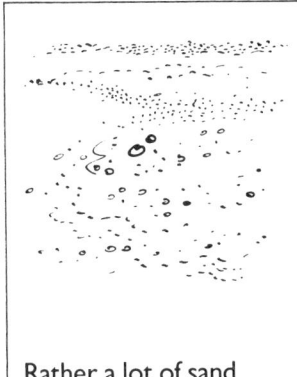 Rather a lot of sand
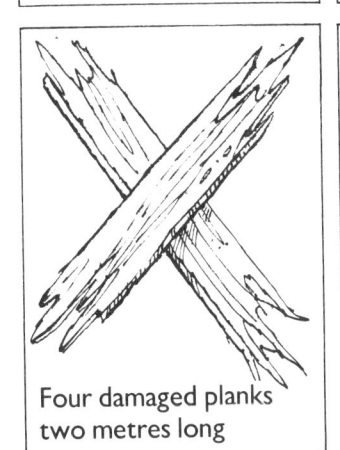 Four damaged planks two metres long	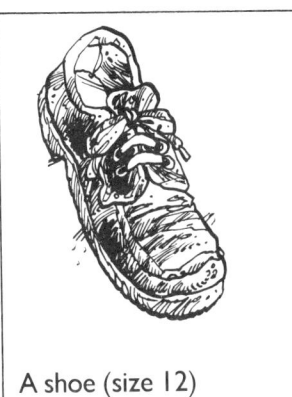 A shoe (size 12)	 The trunk of a palm tree at low water mark	 Shallow cave in the cliff side, 3 metre long × ½ metre deep

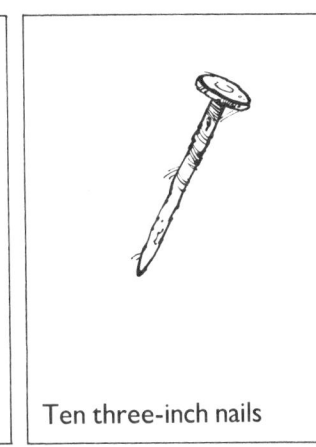

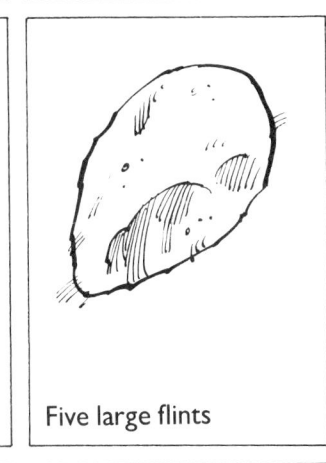

ISLAND 31

ACTIVITY 4

SKILLS
Group decision making, discussion

RESOURCES
Paper

Make a break?

☐ After all that hard work to stay safe and warm, you wake up in your shelter next day to a changed world: a still sky and a clear blue ocean. The tide is low and the great cliffs that held you prisoner now stand some three metres clear of where the sea ripples onto the sand. You walk to the tide's edge and round the cliff wall – to find a long beach with low land behind it, and a little stream trickling across it. Plants grow at the top of the beach, then shrubs, then trees.

And in one of the trees, looking very amused, is one of your crew. Over there, others. In that clearing, a shelter, with packs of food from the wreck which were washed up on the beach.

You join the group. They are clearly discussing something important. Two people are getting impatient.

"Look, I don't care what you say, if we're going to stay alive we'll have to set up some sort of rules."

"Don't see the point. We've got some food, we've got plenty of water – too much, when it pours down like yesterday. This island suits me for a while. It's a change from school with all its 'Do this' and 'Don't do that', so I'm in no hurry to do anything. I'll just swim a little and laze a little and go find some fruit somewhere and maybe fish a little. You can keep your rules."

"Idiot! You don't know what's on this island. You don't know if there's food on it. You don't know anything about it! Who's going to find us? Who's going to know if we're here? What do we do when the food runs out? What do we do when one of us loses our temper? Grow up!"

"You watch it!"

"See what I mean? I want off. That means I stay as long as I need to, to find out how to escape. And if I can't escape I want to find out how I'm getting rescued. You can keep your island. I want out. If anyone feels the same as me we'll need to be organised – and so will you, if you and your lot stay and rot on this lump of a place."

"Where's your sense of adventure?"

"Where's your sense of staying alive?"

☐ The situation is turning nasty. What to do?

1. Decide which group you want to be in.
2. Those who want to stay, produce six sensible arguments for staying and six against trying to escape.
3. Those who want to escape, produce six sensible arguments for leaving and six against staying.

Then everybody can discuss what ought to be done and why.

ACTIVITY 5 — Rules

SKILLS
Decision making, drafting rules, discussion

RESOURCES
Paper

☐ Sorting out whether to try to stay on the island or to escape from it was quite interesting – but the hard fact is that everyone is on the island and is going to have to cope with it.

You do not know how big the island is, whether it can support you or even if it is safe. You do know that you're going to *have* to get on with one another. There won't be time for silly quarrels. You're going to have to be sensible, using rules which everyone can see the sense of obeying.

What are you going to need sets of rules about?

You'll need rules about:
- fair shares – of food, of shelter, of time in discussion
- hygiene
- beach safety
- safety when exploring the island
- keeping watch for rescue
- maintaining any signal systems

You can probably think of other sets of rules you are going to need, to make sure that you work together to survive on the island.

1 With a partner, produce the ten rules for one set which you think is important. Number each rule and keep it brief and clear. Make sure that the most important rules come first, so that they attract readers' attention. You could set out your rules like this example:

> Rules to do with – EXPLORATION
> 1) Never explore the island without letting the rest of the group know which way you are going.
> 2) Never explore the island without a partner being within calling distance.
> 3) Always leave a clear set of signals as you move along, a small pitch of stones, a knotted tuft of grass...

2 Produce your set of rules as a poster. Make it eye-catching.
3 There will be a meeting of the full group at which you will have to defend the set of rules you have created.

ACTIVITY 6

SKILLS
Comprehension

RESOURCES
Instructions on signals, paper

Putting it together

If you are going to be rescued, you will have to make yourself obvious.

How?

One of your group remembers seeing a leaflet on the boat about signalling and thinks that it may have been brought ashore after the shipwreck. It was – well, bits of it were. It's torn and stained, but it could still be useful.

1 Look at the scraps of leaflet on the following pages. Work out the missing bits and patch the scraps together again, so that you can read the leaflet's advice.

SIGNALLING
BASIC FACTS

1. Learn signalling to inform and warn.
2. You can use sound or sight.
   Train in at least two codes.
   In an emergency never give up using your signal system

SIGHT SIGNALS – GROUND

1. Trample a large area flat so that it is clearly human damage.
2. Make an obvious site. a clear or high

   gnalling base on

   big. Use

   Make signs or letters at least six metres rocks or make deep furrows which will cast shadows.
4. Use colours which contrast with the locality.

SIGHT SIGNALS – FIRE

Three fires lit in a triangle are an international disaster sig

Make sure that you have lots of dry material to make smoke by day, flame by night.

For white smoke on a sunny day, add a few green leaves or water lightly. For dark smoke on a dull day, add plastic or lumps of fat.

SIGHT SIGNALS – FLAGS

ake flags which contrast keep them moving.

2. Kites are a good

SIGHT SIGNALS – BOD

with the background colour a[...]
form of flag.

1. Arms out at shoulder level then lowered and raised is the international signal for needing help. Standing with feet apart and arms raised apart = PICK US UP. Standi[ng] with knees bent and arms pointing straight ahead like someone preparing to dive = LAND HERE.

2. Waving a flag vertically in one hand = YES: in an arc [ac]ross the knees = NO.

SIGHT SIGNALS – HELIOGRAPH

1. A mirror, polished tin lid or glossy [...] may work.

2. A signal may work for up to twenty four [...] your rescuers may see you before you [...]

[S]OUND SIGNALS

1. Test metal and wood objects [...] carrying noise.

[...] voice works over

2. Your [...]

3. Your voice [...] calling. Call in [...]

4. Use your voice only when [...] you will be heard.

green leaf [...]

kilometres – so [...] see them.

to see which make the best [...]

medium distances.

is most powerful if you drink before [...] a low booming voice, with your fingers in your ears.

there is a good chance that

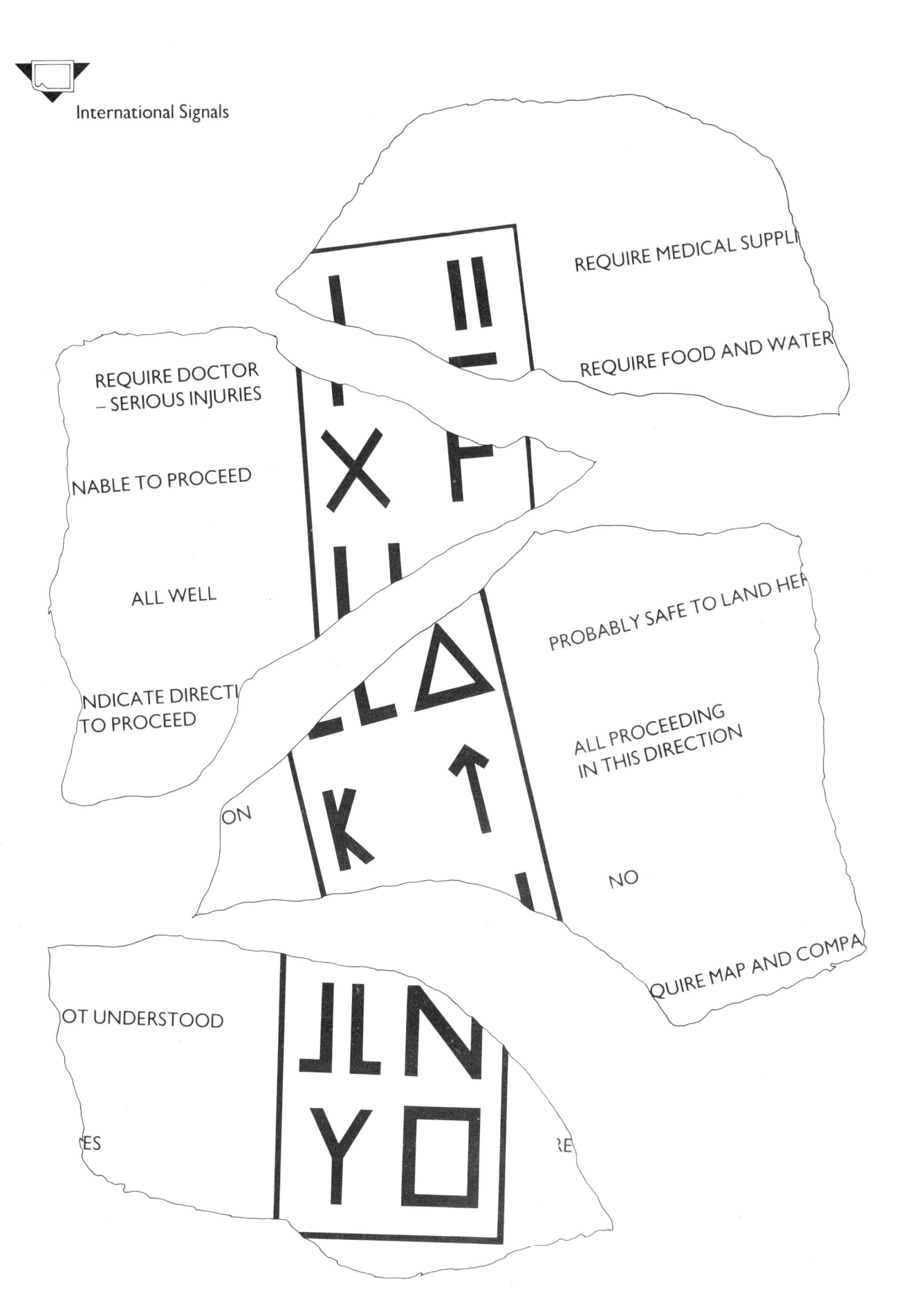

International Signals

REQUIRE MEDICAL SUPPLI[ES]

REQUIRE FOOD AND WATER

REQUIRE DOCTOR
– SERIOUS INJURIES

[U]NABLE TO PROCEED

ALL WELL

[I]NDICATE DIRECTI[ON]
TO PROCEED

PROBABLY SAFE TO LAND HER[E]

ALL PROCEEDING
IN THIS DIRECTION

NO

[RE]QUIRE MAP AND COMPA[SS]

[N]OT UNDERSTOOD

[Y]ES

ACTIVITY 7

SKILLS
Comprehension, working with codes

RESOURCES
Instructions on signals, paper

Help!

☐ Instruction number three in the "Basic facts" section of the leaflet was "Train in at least two codes". Luckily the page with two signalling codes – *Morse* and *Semaphore* – was not damaged.

CODES

	MORSE	SEMAPHORE		MORSE	SEMAPHORE
A	•–		1	•–––	
B	–•••		2	••–––	
C	–•–•		3	•••––	
D	–••		4	••••–	
E	•		5	•••••	
F	••–•		6	–••••	
G	––•		7	––•••	
H	••••		8	–––••	
I	••		9	––––•	
J	•–––		10	–––––	
K	–•–				
L	•–••				
M	––				
N	–•				
O	–––			= number	
P	•––•				
Q	––•–			= erase	
R	•–•				
S	•••				
T	–				
U	••–				
V	•••–				
W	•––				
X	–••–				
Y	–•––				
Z	––••				

1 Work out five basic, brief messages that everyone ought to be able to send in each code if there is a chance of rescue.

VOYAGES: SKILLS IN EVERYDAY ENGLISH

ACTIVITY 8

Mapping the island

SKILLS

Mapping, giving instructions, listening

RESOURCES

Copy of island map (page 40), paper

☐ From the wreck you have a navigation chart which has on it only the outline of the island. Clearly you want to know more. Each person decides to search a different quarter of the island (A, B, C or D). In small groups, you agree on which quarter each person is to explore.

1 Now you are exploring your quarter of the island, *on your own*. Look at the map. It has a list of features and the map symbols for them. Discover five of these features and place the symbols for them on the sites where you discovered them. For example if you found a dangerous beach, put the ! symbol at that place on the map.

DON'T LET ANYONE ELSE SEE WHERE YOU PLACE THEM ON YOUR QUARTER OF THE MAP.

2 Invent signs for two other features you have discovered and sketch those in as well.

Now, back at the camp, get together with the others to fill in the detail of what has been found, pooling your information.

KEEP YOUR MAP CONCEALED. DON'T SHOW IT TO ANYBODY YET. ALL OF YOU *MUST* DESCRIBE WHAT YOU HAVE FOUND, NOT SHOW IT!

3 In turn, each explorer tells the others in the group what he/she has discovered and where. For instance, suppose that the explorer of the "C" quarter discovered a dangerous beach. She/he could say, 'I was right at the top of the island and there were two beaches there, and I almost got trapped by quicksand on the north one.'
You could then pencil the sign for 'Dangerous Beach' where you think the beach is sited on your copy of the map. If an explorer's description is not clear, ask that person to explain again. Carry on until all the explorers have given details of what they have found in their sections of the island.

4 Now compare maps. See how well you have managed to compile an accurate copy by listening to each other without looking at each other's maps.

5 Work on your own, or in a small group, to produce a good copy of the map on a larger scale. Make it as accurate and attractive as possible.

Hill
Mountain
River
Waterfall
Lake

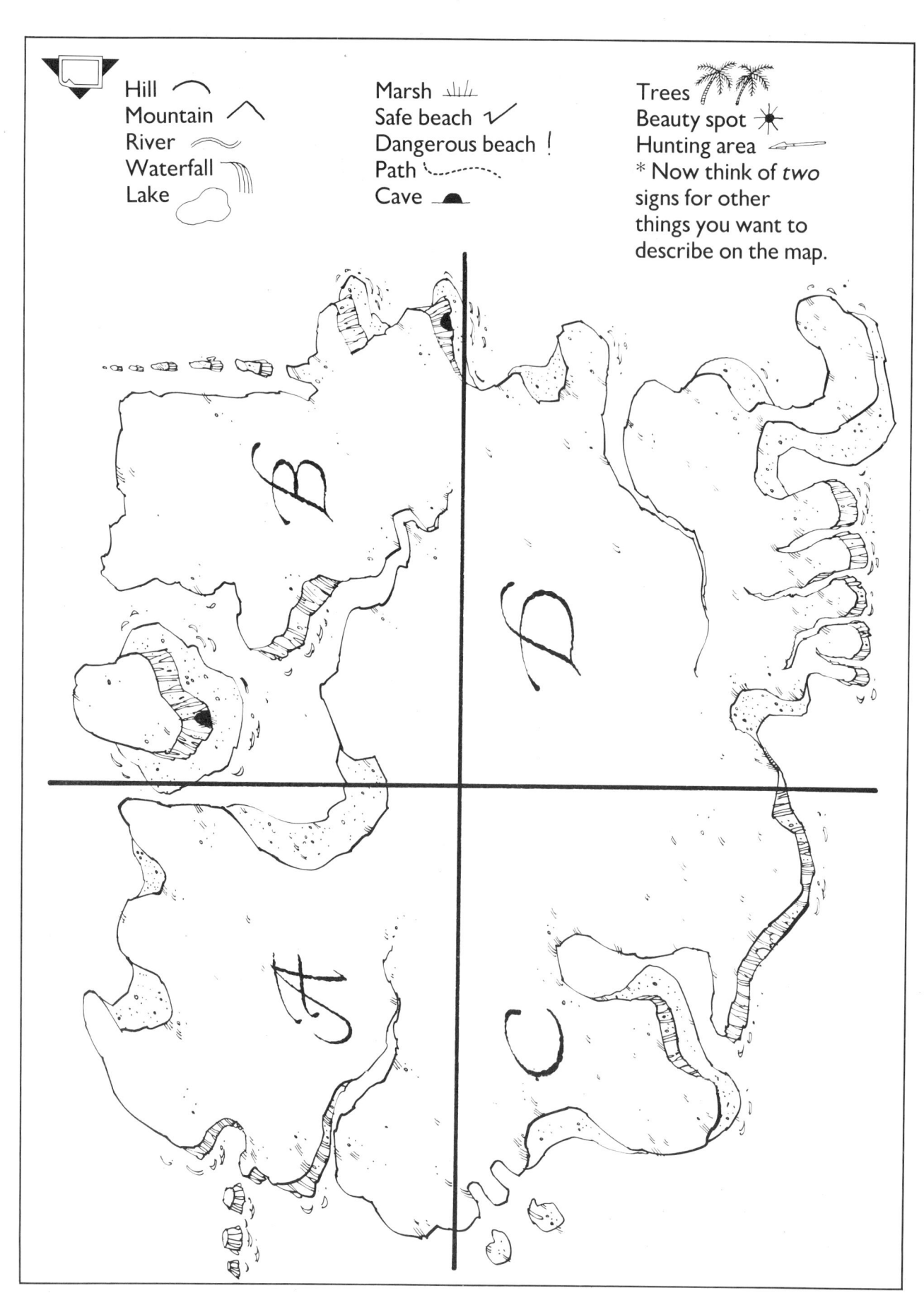

Marsh
Safe beach ✓
Dangerous beach !
Path
Cave

Trees
Beauty spot ✱
Hunting area
* Now think of *two* signs for other things you want to describe on the map.

ACTIVITY 9

Telling the tale

SKILLS
Discussion, note-making, redrafting, writing in paragraphs

RESOURCES
Paper

> "There was something moving around in my part of the island. I thought I saw it a couple of times, but I didn't get a proper look at it. No idea what it was, but it was definitely there."

You were not expecting one of your group to say anything like that. You all went quiet for a minute, not quite sure what to feel or what to say.

> "Better have a look for it – in the morning."

1. As a group, look at your map and decide the route from your shelter to where the creature was seen. The route should take you through or past *three* of the features which you discovered and wrote on the map.

2. Now discuss the hazards you would meet on your journey. They might be:

    - features on your map – such as a quicksand
    - an unexpected event – such as a landslide
    - a drastic change in the weather – such as a hurricane
    - a creature (*not* the one you are trying to find).

    As a group, agree upon the *three* hazards and the order in which you will meet them. Discuss how you could create at least *one* crisis in the account of your journey.

3. Now work on your own to make notes about the hunt for the creature. Take a sheet of lined paper and draw a line down the middle from top to bottom, and another across the middle (side to side) to make four equal boxes. Number them 1, 2, 3, and 4.
    Use the first three of these for notes on your journey, as you meet the three hazards. The fourth is for when you know you are about to meet the creature. Leave that one till last. Each box allows you about five lines of planning for your adventure story.

Use the first three boxes to jot down your ideas, following this recipe

Line 1: the name of the hazard
Line 2: "bare bones" outline of what the journey was like at that point.
Line 3: notes about that hazard – any special words to describe it
Line 4: what you think of it – how it affects you.
Line 5: how you manage to continue on your journey.

ISLAND

For example:

> 1. Swamp.
>
> 2. Waded through swamp for a hundred metres.
>
> 3. Oozy mud – clumps of slimy, dark green grass – evil smell
>
> 4. Swarms of stinging flies – something moving around my feet – panic – unable to scream
>
> 5. Sinking in mud – find palm fronds – hold on to them and pulled out – covered in mud

Fill in the first three boxes in this way.

4 Return to your group. Exchange notes and discuss your versions of what has happened. See if you can agree on who did what on the journey. Revise your notes.

5 Write notes for your fourth and final box as you did for the first three. This is the final stage of your journey when you are creeping up on where you think the creature is. Leave the last sentence as a cliff-hanger – full of suspense as to what will happen next.

6 Using all four boxes of your notes, revise your ideas and write them up as an exciting adventure story in four paragraphs.

ACTIVITY 10

The trap

SKILLS
Linking illustration and writing, creating atmosphere

RESOURCES
Paper

☐ It was quite a journey, but your adventures are not over yet. Do you remember the remark that one of you made?

> "There was something moving around in that part of the island. I thought I saw it a couple of times but I didn't get a proper look at it. No idea what it was, but it was definitely there."

That was what started you on this journey. Your aim is to catch the creature in order to have a look at it. You do not want to harm it, and you want to be able to release it as quickly as you can – with your mutual safety in mind.

1 Look at the part of the island where you think the creature is. What sort of creature could survive there? What would it live on? How would it move? Where would it shelter? What sort of creature wouldn't want you to see it?
You will need to make some intelligent guesses about the creature if you are to trap it. On your own, make your own notes about your creature and draw a sketch.

2 Design a trap to catch the animal. Use the eight items that you did not use when you built your shelter (Activity 3). Draw a clear, labelled diagram of the trap, with precise instructions on how to operate it.

3 Now describe what actually happens as the trap succeeds. Write this final stage of the story of your journey across the island in search of the creature. Describe:

   a building the trap
   b waiting
   c the feelings of intense excitement as the creature nears it
   d the moment the trap works
   e the creature and its reactions
   f its release from the trap and your feelings

ACTIVITY 11

Animal data

SKILLS
Comprehension, producing factual information

RESOURCES
Reference books, paper

☐ The writing in Activity 10 asked you to use all your talents – your imagination, your knowledge of the animal world, your emotions, your ability to invent dramatic description. All of that is fine with an adventure book. It would be dull without it.

There are times when another kind of description is more appropriate. Identification books assume that a reader wants a small amount of essential information, fast. They use:

- a clear, standardised layout, often with sub-sections
- clear, brief descriptions
- clear illustrations or diagrams

1 Find some examples of identification books on animals.

2 Working with a partner, talk about how these books:
   set out their information ("layout")
   use description
   use illustration

3 With your partner, produce an identification aid for each of your creatures. These can be presented *either* like pages from an identification book you have looked at *or* as a wallchart.

ACTIVITY 12

SKILLS
Planning descriptive writing

RESOURCES
Paper

They've seen us!

☐ Being rescued is a matter of luck. It is also a matter of being prepared to give luck a chance to be on your side. That is where your efforts to keep a lookout and maintain a signalling system have been important.

A plane goes overhead.

1 On a piece of paper, show how you would attract its attention.

The plane circles twice and flies off. It may have radioed a message to a ship, for soon you spot smoke on the horizon.

2 Write the message you decide to use to attract the ship if you have a fire or a shiny piece of metal.

The lookout system that your group adopted has succeeded; so has the system your group chose for attracting attention. You've done well! The ship is coming closer.

3 Draw a line down the middle of your page. On the left hand side write notes on what you see as the ship is:

- on the horizon
- still far off
- mid distance but clearly coming towards you
- anchoring outside the reef and lagoon
- launching a small boat which heads through the gap in the reef towards you.

4 Opposite your description of each stage of the ship's approach, write down, in the right hand column, what you do *and* how you feel.

ACTIVITY 13

Rescued!

SKILLS
Making notes, interviewing

RESOURCES
Paper, tape-recorder (optional)

☐ The arrival of your rescuers brings a confusion of emotions, actions, new voices and new people. You ought to try to remember what happened, for this is too important an event to let go.

1. In a small group discuss how you imagine the rescue went, from when the boat came through the reef to when you were taken off the island.

2. Jot down notes on the rescue. Think of this in about four to eight stages and write one line for each.
   You will all need to agree on these events and you will all need a copy of them.

It's amazing how quickly the media arrive on the scene of a good story. It is time to play your part in the story as a rescuer or one of the people who has been rescued, or as an interviewer for a newspaper, or for radio or television. (If you use a tape recorder or video-camera, you may need somebody to concentrate on operating it.)

3. With between two and four people taking part, produce a three minute interview:

   One of you is the interviewer, seeking all the drama and human interest of this event.
   One (or more of you) comes from the rescue ship.
   One (or more of you) has just been rescued.

You have some brief notes on the rescue to work from, but they will not be enough. Get inside your role.

   If you are a reporter, are you a dramatic one or a quiet one as you probe to get a good story?
   If you are a rescuer, how do you feel – triumphant, exhausted, embarassed or . . . ?
   If you have been rescued, what mood are you in and how do you react to these people? Tell of your experience of the rescue.

4. Use the interview as the basis for a two minute radio or television news report or for a front-page article in a newspaper.

5. Have a Welcome Back party. Make a display of all your work and reminisce about your adventure.

Unit 3
Holiday

ACTIVITY 1

SKILLS
Group discussion, oral or written reporting back

RESOURCES
Paper

Action! Holidays!

☐ You are a planning group working for the local Council in the Amenities and Recreation Department. You are involved in promoting the holiday industry in your area.

The planning group has received this memorandum from the Director.

MEMO

From: Director of Amenities & Recreation

Concerning: Tourist Development

To: Staff: Department of Amenities & Recreation

Date: February 29th

   People are increasingly interested in leisure-time activities. Our area will have a great deal to offer visitors if we can develop a new range of such activities. They will create more jobs for local people, bring in more money and provide increased facilities for all of us.

The Amenities Committee asks you to plan a range of activity holidays. These holidays will use local accommodation and the facilities already available. You need to be imaginative in making use of everything that we have in the area – particularly the industrial and commercial parts.

As well as ordinary families, think about specialist groups whom we might attract: for example, foreigners, teenagers, teachers, sports teams.

When you have finished your proposals, you will present a report to the Amenities Committee.

                                        J.D.

---

1. Form Planning Teams of three or four people.
2. Produce a list of as many specialist groups as you can who might be attracted to your area.
3. Discuss activity holidays which you think would appeal to one of these groups. (Do not choose the same group as another Planning Team.)
4. Make a list of these holidays and share your ideas with the other Planning Teams.

ACTIVITY 2

SKILLS
Research, compiling information

RESOURCES
Information sources, paper

What's on offer?

☐ So far you have been thinking about ideal holidays which might appeal to a particular group. Now you need to be more realistic and see what facilities are actually available.

```
M E M O


From:              Director, Amenities and Recreation

Concerning:        Surveying Local Facilities

To:                Planning Teams

Date:              May 1st


Surveying Local Facilities

There are five ways of gathering the information
you need:-

1.   In your Working Party, pool your knowledge
     about places of interest or facilities for
     activity holidays, and make notes about these.

2.   Show your notes to other people who have local
     knowledge and ask their advice.

3.   Contact appropriate local sources of information:
     local council offices, the Tourist Information
     Centre, tourist agencies, firms in the holiday
     trade.  First, ask for information which will
     help fill in pieces missing from your own
     knowledge.  Then ask the experts to suggest
     aspects you might not have thought of already.

4.   Present an outline of what you have discovered
     about local facilities to the other Planning
     Teams.

5.   As you listen to or read other groups' reports,
     add to your own data so that you have a complete
     picture for further use.
```

ACTIVITY 3

SKILLS
Organising

RESOURCES
Copy of Activity Description Form

That special holiday

☐ Your team now has a lot of ideas about people who might want to come to the area for various activity holidays. You also have information about actual facilities.

Now focus your attention on one activity for one set of people – for instance canoeing for families or video-making for people of your own age.

1 Using the layout of the **Activity Description Form,** produce your own form to describe a particular holiday activity and how you could promote it.

Activity Description Form

1 Name of the activity selected..

2 People it could attract..

3 Size of group possible..

4 Facilities already available locally

....

5 Further facilities needed

....

(Explain how these could be provided)

....

6 Number of people needed to run it..

7 Any other information

....

8 Brief outline of events. (Choose either a 3 or a 5 day programme.)

....

---

2 Circulate or display your completed form so that all the Planning Teams know the range of activities being developed.

50 VOYAGES: SKILLS IN EVERYDAY ENGLISH

ACTIVITY 4

SKILLS
Planning a timetable

RESOURCES
Paper

Make their day

☐ You have produced a brief description of a programme for people who would take your Activity Holiday. More detailed planning is needed. Read this example of what a typical day in a programme might look like.

```
                Indoor Archery: Opening day

  9.00    Meet in archery area of gymnasium
          Introduction to instructor

  9.15    Demonstration of equipment
          Talk on safety

 10.00    Demonstration of technique
          First practice session: 15 yards

 10.30    Coffee Break

 11.00    Second practice session: 25 yards

 11.30    Talk on scoring

 12.00    Mini-competition; 25 yards

 12.30    Lunch

  1.30    Film: "Archery in the Olympics"

  2.15    Third practice session: 25 yards (video-taped)

  3.00    Discussion of video-tapes and individual help

  4.00    Team fun competition

  5.00    Break

  6.00    Supper

  7.00    Illustrated talk on "Archery through the Ages"

  8.00    Finish
```

1 Having read this example, discuss the features of one day in *your* programme – the first, the last or one in the middle.
2 Agree on the design of this day and present it as a clear and concise timetable.

HOLIDAY 51

ACTIVITY 5

Holiday school

SKILLS
Field study, note making, report writing

RESOURCES
Copy of Study Holiday Description form, school premises, paper

☐ Read the following memorandum:

```
                        MEMO

From:           Director of Amenities & Recreation

Concerning:     Tourist Development

To:             Planning Teams

Date:           May 5th


The Amenities Committee would like you to consider a
further development: Study Holidays. Schools are
usually empty for the six peak holiday weeks in the
summer – and two weeks at Easter.  Schools are full
of resources to help people learn new skills in
cookery, drama, home crafts, music, science, sports,
technology and so on. How can we use these facilites
to design attractive holidays in which people enjoy
themselves as they learn?
```

1 Choose one kind of Study Holiday which could be based at your school.
2 Survey your school and make notes (including sketches, diagrams and plans where appropriate) on what it has to offer for this particular holiday.
3 Complete your copy of the **Study Holiday Description Form.**
4 Use the form as the basis for a report recommending this holiday and explaining what needs to be done to provide for it in your school.

Study Holiday Description Form

1 Name of the study activity

....

2 People it could attract..

3 Details of facilities already available in the school

    a accommodation

....

    b equipment

....

4 Drawbacks in using the school's facilities as they are now *..

....

* Attach a rough sketch of the school showing the areas which can be used for your study holiday and noting any shortcomings.

ACTIVITY 6

SKILLS
Preparing and presenting a talk

RESOURCES
Previous documents, paper

Planning forum

☐ Now it is time to present your ideas. The whole class is the Amenities Committee and listens to the proposals of the different teams.

Planning Forum

The next meeting of the Amenities Committee will be a forum, and all Planning Teams are to attend.

Each Team is to describe one of its proposals for either Activity or Study Holidays to the full Committee.

After each presentation there will be an open discussion. This will provide time for suggestions which will improve the proposals.

Members of Teams will not be competing against each other. Discussion is intended to bring out the positive side of each Team's proposal and to identify a wide range of Activity and Study Holidays.

---

1 Prepare your proposals to present to the Amenities Committee.
2 Present your proposals when it is your turn.
   Your team should read the advice on GIVING A TALK in SKILLS KIT 5 on page 103 before you prepare your talk.
3 As members of the Amenities Committee, listen to each team's proposals and make constructive comments.
4 Listen to what people say about your proposals and make changes where necessary.

ACTIVITY 7

SKILLS

Decision making, programme design

RESOURCES

Paper, Copy of Events Design Form, (page 56)

Two day holiday

☐ Now that you have studied what your area and your school can provide, you are ready to combine the two. The Amenities Committee has decided to try out a number of "Two Day Speciality Holidays". These will be for families with young people of your age. Some of the time will be based in school learning about the activity; some of the time will be spent in practising it, perhaps in the locality. For instance lessons in sketching might be extended by going on a painting expedition to a local river or canal. Or coaching in football might be followed by a match against a local team and going to see a professional football game.

1 In your team, choose an activity from one of the following areas. Make sure that each team chooses a different activity so that the Amenities Committee can produce a wide and attractive final programme.

- art (e.g. drawing, painting, pottery)
- crafts
- design
- drama and dance
- house crafts
- keep fit activities
- music
- outdoor activities
- science
- team sports (outdoor or indoor)
- technology

2 Produce a two day time-table of events for your activity. Bear in mind:
(i) Each day will last from 9.30 – 4.30 unless there is some special evening event in the locality that you want to build into your programme.
(ii) Leave free time for meals and relaxation.
(iii) Try to make the programme varied, but do not have so many events that people feel rushed.

3 Slot your time-table into the **Events Design form** on the next page.

HOLIDAY

Events Design Form

Time	Place	Activity	Equipment needed

ACTIVITY 8

SKILLS
Planning, drafting a report

RESOURCES
Paper

Making the best of it

☐ People may be keen to take one of the two day holidays on offer, but they may not like being back inside a school. First, they may not find it very attractive. Second, there may not be enough equipment.

You will have to explain to the Amenities Committee what is needed to make these holidays a success.

1 Agree on the area or areas of the school which you want to use.
2 Draw a plan of the area(s). Add notes on what you are satisfied with, what needs to be added, what needs to be converted.
3 List the resources which are already there. List the other resources you would need to make your activity holiday attractive.
4 Using the information from 1, 2 and 3, write a report to the Amenities Committee.

- Explain what your chosen activity is and why you chose it.
- Describe the existing resources.
- Explain what you would like to be developed or altered.
- Give reasons why your proposals should be adopted.

(Use plans, sketches and diagrams to make your report clear.)

Example: Ground Plan of a School Hall

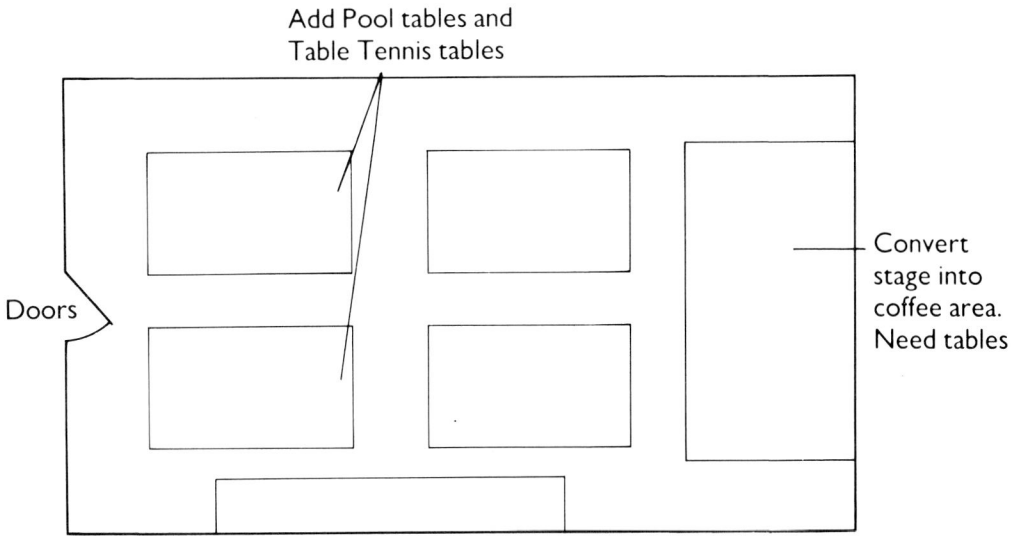

[Diagram of school hall ground plan with annotations: "Add Pool tables and Table Tennis tables" pointing to centre, "Doors" on left, "Convert stage into coffee area. Need tables" on right, "Use kitchen hatch to make food bar." at bottom]

HOLIDAY 57

ACTIVITY 9

SKILLS
Decision making, writing persuasive language

RESOURCES
Art materials, brochures, paper

Publicity brochure

☐ The report you have been writing needed to be clear and brief. Now you have planned your two day activity holiday it is time for your Planning Team to launch a publicity campaign. Advertising is also clear and brief – but it is *lively* as well. See what you can do to attract people.

(You will find advice on ADVERTISING in SKILLS KIT 3 on page 100. If you can, look at some examples of real brochures to get ideas.)

Just remember:

- You are trying to appeal to families which include people of your own age.
- They will want to know what they are going to learn and what they are going to do.
- They will want to feel excited about coming on the holiday.

1 As a team, produce a brochure which people can send for.
   Aim to:
   - tell people what they want to know in clear language
   - use pictures and maps to give information
   - be friendly
   - make the course look attractive

ACTIVITY 10

SKILLS
Decision making, writing persuasive language

RESOURCES
Art materials, tape recorder, paper

Going public

☐ Now you need to advertise your brochure! These advertisements will have to be brief. Advertisements cost money and people don't read through long ones.

1 There are several ways of waking people up to your bright new venture. Choose two from this list which will make people send for your holiday brochure:
- flier (handbill)
- box advertisement
- poster
- local radio advertisement

(You will find advice on ADVERTISING in SKILLS KIT 3 on page 100)

2 Try out several versions. Choose your best two and produce them ready for a final display.

FLIER

LEARN WHILE YOU PLAY!
ACLE ACTIVITY CENTRE
Study Holidays Offer
- Computing
- Swimming
- Tennis
- Archery
- Pottery
- Canoeing

AND LOTS MORE!
Send for your free brochure today!
Acle Activity Centre, Norford, NR3 1AG

POSTER

Do you want to learn new skills?
Are you bored with lying on a beach?
Then come to ACLE ACTIVITY CENTRE

- Swimming
- Tennis
- Computing
- Canoeing
- Archery
- Pottery

AND LOTS MORE!
Send for your free brochure today!
Acle Activity Centre, Norford, NR3 1AG

BOX ADVERTISEMENT

Opening August 1st
ACLE ACTIVITY CENTRE
Fun for all the family
Computing   Archery
Water Sports   Tennis
AND LOTS MORE!
Send for your free brochure today!
Acle Activity Centre, Norford, NR3 1AG

HOLIDAY

ACTIVITY 11

SKILLS
Letter writing

RESOURCES
Paper

Thank you for your enquiry

☐ The Amenities Committee has received the following letters during the year.

> 14 Brook Terrace,
> Stowthwaite,
> Oldham.
>
> 29th December
>
> Director of Amenities,
> Norford Town Council,
> Town Hall,
> Norford.
>
> Dear Sir,
>
> I intend to spend two weeks this summer with my elderly mother who lives in your area. I would like to bring my two children – a boy aged 13 and a girl aged 12 – with me but feel that they would have a more interesting time if they could spend part of the time on a study holiday.
>
> They both like practical craft activities. Do you have summer programmes for people of their age, offering a variety of activities which they would enjoy?
>
> I would be grateful if you would send me details of anything of this kind that your area can offer.
>
> Yours faithfully,
>
> H. Craggs

251, Entwood Rd,
Cringleton,
Winsford NF9 6AW.
Tel: 959163

23rd December

Director of Amenities,
Norford Town Council,
Town Hall,
Norford.

Dear Sir,

Each year my wife and I choose a different part of the country for a brief holiday. We like to be outdoors and we have enjoyed walking tours and learning how to sketch.

This year we would like to visit your area and, if possible, we would like to join a group which is involved in some outdoor activity.

Our children are in their early teens. They would like an active holiday with a sporting flavour, which includes coaching.

I would be most grateful if you could forward any information which you have available on holidays of this kind in your area.

Yours faithfully,
R. J. Entwhistle

1 In your team, discuss these questions:
- How can you help?
- Which activity holidays fit the bill?
- How can you interest the letter writers in what you are offering?

Look at SKILLS KIT 2 on page 98.

2 On your own, write a reply to one of the letters.
3 Meet as a team to compare letters and draw up a list of what makes a good reply.

ACTIVITY 12

SKILLS
Display, formal oral reporting

RESOURCES
Previous written work, paper

Publicity launch

Now is the time to draw together all your material and present it to the whole class at a publicity launch.
You will be presenting your outlines for:
- activity holidays
- descriptions of resources available and needed
- publicity material.

```
                          MEMO

From:         Secretary, Council Public Relations Committee

Concerning:   Publicity Launch

To:           Planning Teams

Date:         July 15th


You are invited to a reception to launch your proposals for activity holidays in
the area.

I would like to explain to you how the event will be run.

Your Planning Team will be able to make an uninterrupted presentation of its
ideas, followed by time for discussion with the guests.

It will be more enjoyable if your presentation is based upon visual evidence
such as drawings, charts and/or photographs, which your Team can explain to
everyone else at the Reception. Each member of the Team should describe a
particular aspect of your project.

It will be helpful if your Team has a Presentation Leader to introduce the
members of the Team, give a brief summary of each member's role and generally
link together the whole presentation, before summing it up.

I am instructed by the Committee to thank you for all your hard work on this
project. I hope that after the presentation of your proposals there will be
time for everyone to look at the exhibits more informally.
```

1 A publicity launch tries to be as attractive and exciting as possible. Work with your teacher to produce a grand event.

Unit 4
Scan

ACTIVITY 1

SKILLS
Decision making, reporting

RESOURCES
Copy of report form (page 65), paper

Team up with SCAN

- How well do you know your neighbourhood – the area where you live?
- How well do you know your community – the people who live in it?
- How can you help others to know it better?

> JOIN **SCAN** –
> **S**HARING **C**OMMUNITY **A**ND **N**EIGHBOURHOOD.
>
> FORM A **SCAN TEAM**.
> EXPLORE YOUR NEIGHBOURHOOD.
> SHARE YOUR KNOWLEDGE WITH OTHERS.

SCAN is your chance to find out a little more about where you live and to make practical use of that information, by telling others who need it.

You will be asked to provide information for newcomers to the area in one of these age groups:
1 the 8 – 14 age group
2 the 65 – 75 age group

If your group prefers to choose another age group, talk to your teacher about it.

SCAN information should be interesting and genuinely useful. The success of your SCAN project depends on you.

SCAN has five stages:

1. MAPPING THE NEIGHBOURHOOD – using and making maps in order to understand the locality.
2. EXPLAINING SCAN – working out how to make SCAN better known in the locality.
3. TALKING WITH THE COMMUNITY – collecting further information about the locality from people who live in it.
4. MAKING SENSE TOGETHER – organising further information before publishing it.
5. USING THE LOCALITY – publishing the information for newcomers to use.

1. Form a team and discuss which age group you want to inform about your neighbourhood. Work out three reasons for your choice.
2. List the sorts of information these newcomers might need.
3. As a group, compose a brief list of what you intend to do, and present it to the other SCAN groups. Follow the format on the next page.

REPORT FORM

SCAN TEAM: Members ....
....
....
....

Age group chosen..

Reasons for choosing this age group:

1 _____
2 _____
3 _____

Information this group may need to know:

1 _____
2 _____
3 _____
4 _____
5 _____
6 _____
7 _____
8 _____
9 _____
10 _____

Where we think we could obtain information and advice for our SCAN project:

1 _____
2 _____
3 _____
4 _____
5 _____

ACTIVITY 2

SKILLS
Map reading, making notes

RESOURCES
Large scale map of your area, paper

Finding out

1. In your team, look at a large scale map of your area and work out where you are on it.
2. Look at the symbols which it uses. (Ask your teacher for help if you do not understand them.) The symbols show you where roads and buildings are. You can see if there is a church or a railway station. If you are using a large scale Ordnance Survey map, you can even see if there are footpaths and electricity pylons.
3. As a team, see what else this part of the map tells you about your neighbourhood. This section of the map shows you some of the details that your chosen age-group might need to know, but it does not show them all: where to find the baker's, or bus stops or the video hire centre or the dentist's.
4. Work on your own. Draw two columns on a sheet of rough paper. In the left hand column, list information on your map which will be useful to people in the chosen age group. In the right hand column, list information which you think someone in your age group is going to need which is not on the map.
5. Meet the rest of your team. Bring together everyone's information. Set it out in two columns as before.
6. Look at the right hand column. Where will you find the missing information? Who can help you?

- parents
- Town Hall
- friends
- neighbours
- Tourist Bureau
- Citizens Advice Bureau
- bus or railway station
- and... ???

7. Working as a team, decide which people you think will be able to help you. Write out the questions you would like to ask them. Show these to your teacher for advice. Can you go on to find out the information?

ACTIVITY 3

SKILLS
Illustration, justification of decisions

RESOURCES
Logos, drawing materials, paper

Go for a logo

☐ Imagine that the Local Director of another SCAN Project has sent you this memorandum.

```
                        MEMO
FROM:        LOCAL DIRECTOR, SCAN

SUBJECT:     EXPLAINING SCAN

TO:          LOCAL SCAN COMMITTEE


SCAN needs to persuade people that it is a useful
project. That will partly depend on making sure that
we explain it clearly and that we make it attractive.

Our first task is to design a "logo" - a symbol that
people link with the project. A logo has to be
adaptable, so you can reproduce it as a small or
large-scale logo on:

        part of a large poster
        a letter heading
        a tee-shirt
        a badge
```

1. As a team, collect logos from:
   - magazines
   - publishers' logos in/on books
   - trademarks on clothing/other possessions
   - badges and emblems
   - transport systems' emblems

2. Discuss what you like or do not like about ten of them.
3. Work on your own. Design a possible logo to make SCAN known in your **locality.** Present your logo as a sketch approximately 15cms by 20cms. Write an explanation of what you want it to suggest and how you want it to appeal to people in 50 to 100 words. Make sure that your logo and commentary are clear enough to be put on display.
4. Meet as a team and decide on the best design.
5. Present your winning design and the reasons for choosing it to other teams. Select just one logo for the whole project.

ACTIVITY 4

SKILLS
Decision making, illustration

RESOURCES
Letter-head examples, paper

Headed paper

☐ Imagine that you have received the following letter from a printing firm.

BARBOUR PRESS,
Gilson Street,
Upton.

Dear SCAN Committee,

I understand that you have formed a SCAN team in your locality. Often you will make your first contact with people through a letter. A well-presented letter on the project's own headed paper is most likely to interest its reader.

We at Barbour Press will be happy to produce your SCAN project's headed paper. I enclose some examples of headed paper. The following points are worth considering as you look at them:-

a) What is the immediate impression of this letterhead? Is it adventurous and bold or modest or stylish or what?

b) Is there a logo? If so, where is it sited? What is it trying to tell us?

c) What words are printed on the paper? What do they tell us? What sort of print is used? Is it simple or ornate, dignified or lively? Is some of the print bigger than the rest? Why?

I hope that you will find this information of use as you decide upon your own letter-heading.

Yours faithfully,

C Axton

C Axton
Managing Director

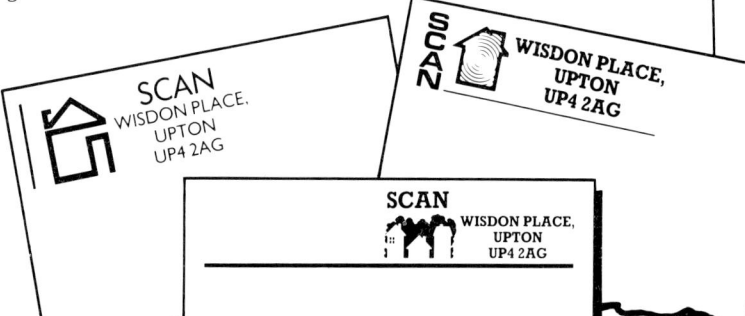

---

1. As a team, look at the samples and discuss what you like about them.
2. Design a printed letter head, complete with your logo, which you think best represents your project and which will be attractive to its readers.
3. Meet as a class to decide upon a final choice which could be duplicated for use.

ACTIVITY 5

SKILLS
Condensing information, letter writing

RESOURCES
Headed paper, card, paper

Making introductions

☐ It is time for teams to add to their knowledge of the area by talking to people and getting further information. That means producing two important documents:

- an identification card
- a letter asking for help

IDENTIFICATION CARD

> SCAN
>
> David Smith
> Denton School
> Wisdom Place
> Upton UP4 2AY

This document has to:

a say who you are and why you are investigating the area to gather information.
b explain that you are seeking help from people in the area and that they should contact your teacher if they would like any further information.

It also needs to be well-presented, polite and *brief*.

1 As a team, produce the first draft of *your* identification document and present it to your teacher.
2 Once it has been cleared, produce a final version for your teacher to countersign. If you are able to go out to interview, you can carry this with you.

LETTER

1 Produce a draft of a letter to a particular person who can help you with your enquiries about the area. Keep it clear and brief. (You will find advice on LETTER WRITING in SKILLS KIT 2 on page 98 useful.)
2 Show this draft to your teacher before taking any further action. You might be able to send it.

ACTIVITY 6

SKILLS
Analysing an interview, creating guidelines

RESOURCES
Paper

Sorry, I'll ask that again!

Much of your information is likely to come from interviewing people. You need to talk to people in the community. People will often help you, provided that you are well prepared and pleasant. Imagine that you overheard this disastrous interview!

(I = Interviewer)
(M = person being interviewed)

I: I'm at school and they said I've got to go and interview somebody old.

M: What did you say?

I: I said that I've got to talk to somebody who's getting on, 'cos we're doing some work on what you need to know about living around here.

M: I'm not old! I'm only seventy!

I: That's older than me, but anyhow, we're doing a project on the community and I want to ask you some questions.

M: I don't know who you are. Who said you could do this?

I: I'm a pupil at the High School. All I want is you to answer some simple questions. That's all you've got to do, and that'll only take you a couple of minutes. It's not difficult, or anything like that.

M: (Silence)

I: Look, here's the first one. Where do other old people live around here?

M: They live all over. They're like everybody else.

I: That's a bit vague.

M: Well, it happens to be true. What are you trying to find out? It's not very clear to me.

I: Just want to see if you're everywhere or if you live in special places – old people's homes and that sort of thing.

M: Well I don't! I'm not that old! But there is an old people's home in Restwell Avenue.

I: O.K. What are your most important routes?

M: What d'you mean, roots?

I: You know – where you travel most often.

M: Well, there's the 87 bus up to the Talitha Centre for my main shopping . . .

I: Hang on! Don't go so fast. I've got to take notes.

M: Well, I go to the Centre, but I still like going to Green's.

I: Where's that?

M: Just around the corner from here.

I: What for?

M: For anything else I need, you know, if I run out of anything.

I: What sort of things? What sort of shop is Green's?

1 Discuss where the interviewer was making mistakes in that transcript.
2 Produce a clear and brief list of ten points of advice on how to conduct a pleasant and useful interview.

ACTIVITY 7 — Checklist

SKILLS
Interviewing, note-making

RESOURCES
Copies of checklist, paper

☐ Obtaining information during an interview or a talk is fairly easy. Remembering it or writing it down is not. Use a **checklist** to make sure you cover all the questions you want to ask. A good checklist leaves you two or three lines after each item in which to write notes about people's answers. You can use this information later to write your SCAN leaflet.

Below is a checklist to use in preparing your questionnaire for interviewing people about how they *use* the locality.

Use copies of this checklist to interview at least three people in the age group that you are studying. (You will find advice on MAKING NOTES in SKILLS KITS 1 on page 96) This will help you draw up your questionnaire.

CHECKLIST FOR INTERVIEWING USERS OF THE LOCALITY
1 Where do people of your age range live in the locality?
2 What are your most important travel routes in the locality?
3 Where do you shop?
4 Where do you go for education?
5 Where do you go for entertainment?
6 Where do you go for health care?
7 Where do you go to meet people?
8 Are there any other places especially for your use?
9 What other places in the locality are important to you?
10 Is there any other information about using the locality that would help people of your own range?

ACTIVITY 8

Asking questions

SKILLS
Designing questionnaires, choosing appropriate language

RESOURCES
Paper

☐ As a team, produce questionnaires for use with three different *providers*. (For instance, a doctor *provides* health services, the owner of a grocery van *provides* food services, and so on.) Some questions could be asked of any provider. Some may apply to a particular provider.

For example, you might think of these as interesting topics to ask a shop owner or manager.

- What do you sell?
- Which are your most popular items?
- What are your opening hours?
- When are the busiest/quietest times to shop?
- Do you have a delivery service?
- Who are your customers?
- Do you give advice to your customers?

You cannot ask questions as brusquely as this so you and your team will need to work out more polite ways of seeking what you want to know. Bear this is mind as you produce and use your questionnaires.

(You will find advice on DESIGNING QUESTIONNAIRES in SKILLS KIT 6 on page 104)

ACTIVITY 9

SKILLS
Collating information

RESOURCES
Paper, interview information

Sorting information

1 After you have conducted your interviews, use the layout of the form below to organise what you have found out about how people *use* the locality. Remember that you are sorting out your information in order to publish it – so organise it clearly.

	INTERVIEWEE 1	INTERVIEWEE 2, etc
HOME BASE		
ROUTES AND TRANSPORT		
SHOPPING		
HEALTH CARE		
ENTERTAINMENT		
SOCIAL CENTRES		
ADDITIONAL INFORMATION FOR NEWCOMERS		

2 As a team, design and use your own form for organising information from your interviews with *providers*.

ACTIVITY 10

SKILLS
Presentation skills

RESOURCES
Paper

Choose your format

☐ So far you have been gathering information in order to produce a publication called USING YOUR LOCALITY.
You have had to think about:

1 The age range you are writing for.
2 The information you think will be of help to newcomers in that age range.

Now you have to think about:

3 The best way of presenting your information.

Information is often produced as a leaflet. That is an economical and simple way of publishing it – but there are others.

Imagine that you have received the proposals of these two printers.

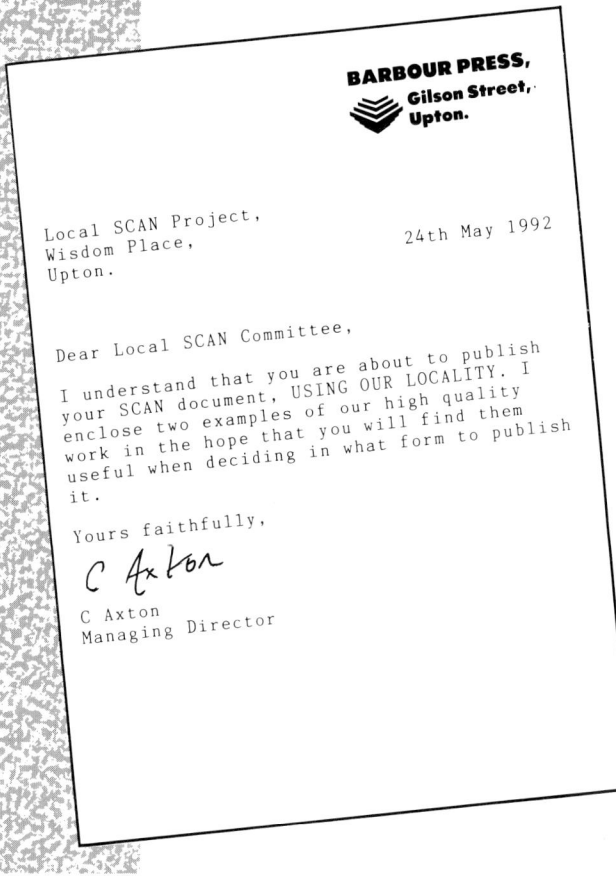

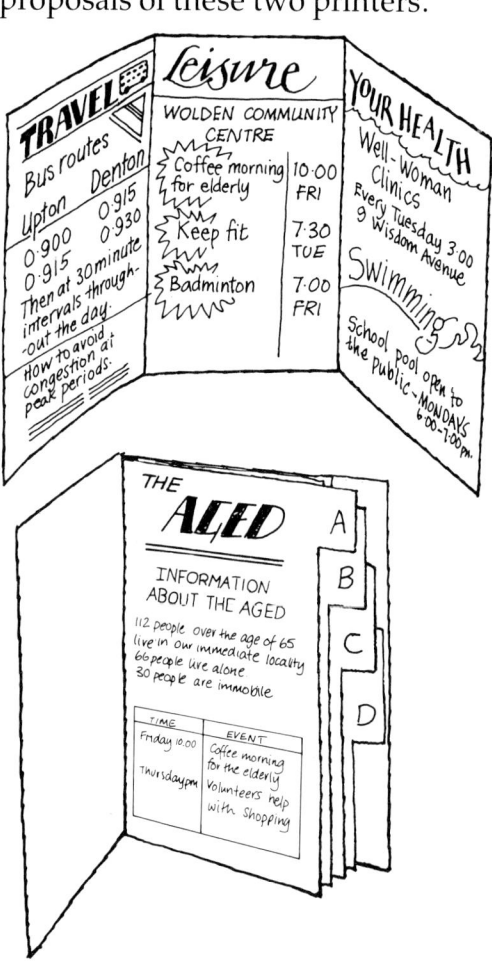

BARBOUR PRESS,
Gilson Street,
Upton.

Local SCAN Project,
Wisdom Place,
Upton.

24th May 1992

Dear Local SCAN Committee,

I understand that you are about to publish your SCAN document, USING OUR LOCALITY. I enclose two examples of our high quality work in the hope that you will find them useful when deciding in what form to publish it.

Yours faithfully,

C Axton

C Axton
Managing Director

TRAVEL
Bus routes
Upton Denton
0·900   0·915
0·915   0·930
Then at 30 minute intervals throughout the day.
How to avoid congestion at peak periods.

Leisure
WOLDEN COMMUNITY CENTRE
Coffee morning for elderly — 10·00 FRI
Keep fit — 7·30 TUE
Badminton — 7·00 FRI

YOUR HEALTH
Well-Woman Clinics
Every Tuesday 3·00
9 Wisdom Avenue
Swimming
School pool open to the public – MONDAYS 6·00–7·00pm.

THE AGED A
INFORMATION ABOUT THE AGED
112 people over the age of 65 live in our immediate locality
66 people live alone
30 people are immobile

TIME	EVENT
Friday 10.00	Coffee morning for the elderly
Thursday pm	Volunteers help with shopping

B
C
D

74 VOYAGES: SKILLS IN EVERYDAY ENGLISH

Do you want to know who can print scan? We can!

JACKDAW PRESS
Pride Road, Upton.

If you want people to scan your scan then we're the people who ought to scan it first!

How about this for a change? The 'using your locality' pack of cards! On the back of each card you'll find items in big print – food shops, cinemas, open spaces – and on the other all you need to know about them. Each card is numbered and there's an index on the pack's outside. Great fun! Great idea!!

Or how about our **foldaway mapsheet**? The map is in the middle of the mapsheet and round the edge is all the information any newcomer will need. It's neat and simple.

1. Draw up a checklist like this one to compare the suggestions in the two letters.

TYPE OF PUBLICATION	POINTS FOR	POINTS AGAINST
TRIPTYCH FOLDER		
TOPIC BOOKLET		
PACK OF INFORMATION CARDS		
FOLDAWAY MAPSHEET		

2. Decide on how you want to present your publication called USING OUR LOCALITY. Write an explanation to be presented to your teacher.

ACTIVITY 11

Sharing SCAN

SKILLS

Choosing publication styles, publishing factual information

RESOURCES

Examples of local information materials, resources for publishing, paper

It's time to publish. So far, you have:
- thought about the information that newcomers of a particular age group might need.
- practised the skills needed when you are interviewing people for information.
- practised sorting out what information to include and how to present it.
- thought about various ways of publishing information so that people will read it and make use of it.

Now you need to go into more detail. Look at examples of brochures, leaflets, pamphlets and maps available in your area. Look at how they help you to find information in them. Think about:

1. How they use pictures, maps, sketches, illustrations of all kinds – to break up the print, make it look more attractive and the meaning stand out more clearly.
2. How they keep the text brief and to the point. They know that readers do not want to read 100 words when 10 words or a brief reference to a map would tell them what they wanted to know at a glance.
3. How they make the information look attractive – using colour, clear layout, and symbols – using different styles of type for headlines.

   You can use these features to make the reader look at the most important information first.

1. As a team, decide on the features which you think would attract your readers and to use these in your publications.
2. Now it's time for you to publish your material. Use pencils, felt-tipped pens, card – whatever you need to produce the best results. You might be able to use a word-processor in order to draft, revise and print professional-looking text. Keep on working as a team and keep in touch with your teacher.
3. If you can, arrange for your PUBLICATION to be displayed in the classroom. Better still, arrange for it to be presented to people in the age group you have been working for.

GOOD LUCK!

Unit 5
Radio Wideawake

ACTIVITY 1

SKILLS
Letter writing

RESOURCES
Paper

Answering an advertisement

☐ When you listen to local radio, you might have wondered what it is like to make a programme. Imagine that you saw this advertisement in the local paper:

Radio WIDEAWAKE

WANTED: Dynamic, creative young people to train as Producers and Production Staff for **RADIO WIDEAWAKE**, a new and developing local radio station. Must be well-motivated, with initiative, and new ideas. Detailed knowledge of local radio output and willingness to specialise in a particular type of programme an advantage.

Write with brief details and demonstration tape to

Station Manager,
RADIO WIDEAWAKE,
William Cotton House,
715 Tempus Rd.,
Upton.

1 Write a letter to the Station Manager saying that you are interested in applying, and will make a demonstration tape with the help of some friends.

You will find advice on WRITING LETTERS in SKILLS KIT 2 on page 98 helpful.

ACTIVITY 2

SKILLS
Comprehension, analysis

RESOURCES
Local newspaper, paper

Exploring radio programmes

☐ You need to do some research into what a local radio station produces. Look at this extract from the Radio & TV Guide page of a local paper, and compare it with one from your own area.

1. Working with a partner, compare the types of programmes your local station actually produces with Radio Wideawake's programme schedule below.
2. Make written notes on the similarities and differences between the two stations.
3. Compare your findings with another pair and produce a list which shows:

   - the kinds of programme you have found
   - the kinds most frequently broadcast
   - the kinds least frequently broadcast

   - which are given a brief time-slot
   - which are given extended time
   - which are for a special time of day
   - which are for a particular group of people.

RADIO WIDEAWAKE

6.30 GET UP 'N' GO SHOW – latest pop music hosted by your own Jimmy "Disc" Turner with his zappy, zany style.

8.30 NOW WHO'S TALKING? – community news and views.

9.00 MORNING ROUND UP – news, current affairs, magazine features, sports round up.

10.00 ON CALL – your music request show with phone-in competitions and conversations.

11.00 ROUND AND ABOUT – this week the R & A team visit another mystery local place, giving a profile of it past and present, interviewing local people and playing their record requests.

12.00 MID-DAY – national and international news, weather.

12.30 REGIONAL NEWS and current affairs.

1.00 AFTERNOON ACTION – variety programme with features on gardening, cookery, DIY. (Sponsored by Hall's DIY superstore)

2.00 ON OUR STREET – popular soap opera.

2.30 STAR SHAPE – in-depth study of a personality in entertainment (music, radio, television) with extracts of their work.

3.00 ON THE MOVE – popular music hosted by D.J. Bill Etherington. News flashes every 15 minutes.

4.00 TIME FOR A TALE – serial reading of Jane Driscoll's "Desert Adventure".

4.30 SCHOOL'S OUT – the busy variety programme for younger listeners, with the latest on pop, sports, hobbies and pastimes.

6.00 NEWS – National and international news and weather.

7.00 OVER TO YOU – local talent competes for your votes. Listen in and phone in.

8.00 RED HOT – up to the minute music and news from the pop scene.

10.00 NEWS ROUND UP

10.05 GHOSTS AND GHOULS – tonight's spooky drama "Into the dark tower".

10.30 LATE 'N' LAZY SHOW – easy to listen to music with your relaxed hostess, Annie Williamson.

12.00 FINALE – review of the major news stories of the day, previews of tomorrow's programmes.

RADIO WIDEAWAKE

ACTIVITY 3

What sort of programme?

SKILLS
Analysis, decision making

RESOURCES
Copy of Programme Analysis Sheet, paper

☐ Radio needs to catch and hold your attention. It can do this by using a variety of types of programme. It can also use a wide range of techniques.

You may have found in your lists some of these types of programme:

- advertising
- competitions
- documentary
- drama
- features
- interview
- magazine
- music
- news
- panel game
- phone-in
- reading

You may also have noticed some of these techniques:

- recorded or live material
- studio or outside broadcast
- music, sound effects
- commentary (one person), dialogue (two people) discussion (several people).

1. Form a production team of about four people to plan a demonstration tape for Radio Wideawake.
2. As a team, decide on a type of programme which interests you and which you would like to make.
3. Discuss your plans with the other groups so that overall your class produces a balanced day of programmes.
4. Listen to at least one example of your type of programme on the radio, and use the **Programme Analysis Sheet** to help you to work out how this type of programme is constructed.

Programme Analysis Sheet

Type of programme..
Name of programme ....
Time of broadcast ....
How often broadcast? ....
Music used and how? ....

Name of main presenter/host...
Name of other presenters ....
Number of other performers...
Type of performers...

Number of Guests involved..
Type of Guests...

Time based in Studio (%)...
Time spent in Outside Broadcast (%) ....

Sound effects used and how?

Description of contents:
Part 1

Part 2

Part 3

Part 4

Part 5

Evaluation

Whole programme interesting or only parts?

Which parts were best?

Any performer particularly good?
Why?

Any interesting techniques?

Any improvements you could suggest?

ACTIVITY 4

SKILLS
Decision making

RESOURCES
Paper

Which part is yours?

☐ Four sorts of people help to make a programme.

1. Read the descriptions below.
2. As a group decide which of these roles will be necessary in your proposed programme.
3. On your own, list which of these roles interest you and might suit you.

1 PRODUCTION – staff who write and record the material. They work in teams under the leadership of a Producer to:

- plan the programme
- research the material
- write the script

2 TECHNICAL – staff who handle the recording equipment. They need to know how the programme is to be made so that:

- before the recording they advise Production on what is possible.

Their job is also to check that:
- the equipment is working correctly
- the studio is set out correctly
- any pre-recorded material (records, taped interviews and advertisements) is ready.
- They record the broadcast.
- If they have the time and equipment, they edit tapes.

3 PERFORMERS – people who might take part in the programme:

- Host – introduces programme and links parts together
- Presenters – take charge of parts of the programme
- Interviewers
- Actors in drama, sketches, serials
- Disc jockey
- News readers
- Reporters

4 GUESTS – people taking part without a script:

- Members of the public being interviewed
- Experts with special knowledge
- Quiz show participants
- Pop stars and celebrities

ACTIVITY 5

Interviewing

SKILLS
Interviewing

RESOURCES
Copy of Programme Credits Sheet, letters from Activity 1, paper

☐ You have decided what sort of programme you want to produce and which roles are necessary. You will be interviewing members of your group for these roles.

As a group, consider one role at a time:

1 Decide what skills are needed for this role.
2 Make a list of questions which could be asked to find out who in your group has those skills.
3 Decide whether a test of some kind will help to find how competent someone is.
  (A test might be reading aloud a passage from a story or the headlines from a newspaper – making up a commentary on some event – making a brief tape-recording – so that you can compare performances. Don't just take someone's word that they are good at something!)
4 Now interview each person, making use of:
  • the list of questions about each role
  • the letter that each person wrote to the Station Manager of Radio Wideawake
  • paper on which to make notes about the answers.
5 After the interviews, the group should discuss who would be best in each of the roles that the programme needs. Everyone is likely to take on more than one role.
6 Once the group has agreed on roles, fill in the **Programme Credits** sheet.

Programme Credits

Producer ....
Planners ....
  ....
Researchers ....
  ....
Scriptwriters ....
  ....
Technical staff ....
  ....

People taking on other roles (Host/Presenters/Interviewers/Actors/Disc jockey/News readers):

Name .... role ....
Name .... role ....
Name .... role ....
Name .... role ....
Name .... role ....
Name .... role ....

RADIO WIDEAWAKE

ACTIVITY 6

Getting going

SKILLS

Planning, consultation

RESOURCES

Copy of completed **Programme Analysis Sheet,** copy of Programme Proposal Form, paper

☐ Now your group is a Production Team. Begin to plan your demonstration tape of a programme in detail, starting with the shape that it is to take.

1. Refer back to your **Programme Analysis Sheet.** This will remind you of the different parts that made up the type of programme which you studied. It will help you to construct a programme of the same type.
2. Discuss in what ways your programme is going to be the same or different.
3. Produce an outline plan for the demonstration tape of your programme which you are going to send to Radio Wideawake. You need to think about:

   length
   signature tune
   introduction
   component parts
   linking commentary
   slots between parts
   advertisements
   conclusion

(You will find further information on designing a programme in SKILLS KIT 8, THE BROADCASTER'S TRAINING MANUAL page 107.)

4. Discuss your draft plan with other groups and make any necessary changes.
5. Complete the **Programme Proposal Form.**

84 VOYAGES: SKILLS IN EVERYDAY ENGLISH

Programme Proposal Form

Type of Programme ....

Name of Programme..

Description of contents:

Part 1

Part 2

Part 3

Part 4

Part 5

Effects

Music/Sound effects needed

Pre-recorded material:

Item 1..

Item 2..

Outside Broadcast ....

ACTIVITY 7

SKILLS
Information gathering, consultation

RESOURCES
Information sources, Programme Proposal Form, paper

Something to talk about

☐ You need to gather information for your programme. For instance, the DJ of a pop music show needs to research the backgrounds of the performers, the current music scene and any other interesting snippets that will keep listeners listening. Interviewers will need to prepare questions which can be answered by the person they are interviewing. Items for news and advice programmes must be checked for accuracy . . . and so on.

Sometimes you will need to go to the library to check facts in reference books, biographies, information books.
(See SKILLS KIT 7, READING FOR INFORMATION on page 106.)
Often you will find information by talking with people.

Wherever you get your information from, you need to make notes. (See SKILLS KIT 1 page 96 on MAKING NOTES.)

1 Using your completed **Programme Proposal Form,** discuss the content of your programme and decide what you need to find out.

2 Divide the content into parts so that each of you can be responsible for collecting part of the information.

3 Meet frequently to check progress.

ACTIVITY 8

The script

SKILLS

Writing sections of a script

RESOURCES

Completed Programme Proposal form, paper

☐ When you are writing a programme you need to decide when to use "full script" and when to use "semi-script".

FULL SCRIPT

Some parts of a programme may be "fully scripted" – every word has been written down to be read out by the speaker. A speaker on the radio cannot be seen and so it is not important to hide the script. But listeners do not like it if it sounds as if you are reading. If you use "full script" it must be written to sound like natural speech when it is read out.

For instance in a book we might write:

Consider the arguments in favour of the construction of a new swimming pool by the Council on the recently purchased land adjoining the Newhay High School.

If you read that out loud it sounds very formal and not at all like spoken English. A more natural way of saying the same thing would be:

The Council has just bought a plot of land next to the Newhay High School and intends to build a new swimming pool there. What are the arguments in favour of the plan?

An even more informal style would be:

Have you heard about the new swimming pool? Well the Council has just bought some land next to Newhay High School and that's where they want to build it. Why do you think they think that is the right spot?

All these three examples have been written down, but the last two sound more like ordinary spoken English when read aloud. Radio scripts need to help their readers sound as if they are speaking naturally and without a script.

The fully scripted parts of a programme are the safe parts. You know what is going to be said, that it makes sense and that it will fit the time allowed exactly. As long as the person reading does not lose the place then these parts of the programme cannot go wrong!

SEMI-SCRIPT

Some parts of a radio broadcast may be only "semi-scripted".

- Interviews may use fully scripted questions, but the answers are what the speaker wants to say at that time. It would sound artificial to have scripted answers in an interview.
- A commentary on a football match cannot be scripted at all, though commentators will have many favourite phrases to describe a good pass or an impressive goal. They also do a lot of research into the background of teams and players and will have these facts in front of them, to slot in during the game.
- Often a talk show will hold a kind of rehearsal before the broadcast, when the interviewer talks with the guest and finds out what kinds of things the visitor is likely to say. The questions and prompts are then written semi-scripted so that the interview will bring out the best in the guest.

A script needs to show:
1 Who does what.
2 What is said.

For instance, a news magazine programme might look like this, with full and semi-scripting.

```
TAPE 1:   (Signature tune: fade-out.  20 seconds.)

HOST J.D.:  Good morning and welcome to "Morning Roundup" presented by me, John
Dawson, and Hilary Tindle.  This morning we have an interview in the studio with
sports personality, Tricia Matthews, followed by a report on new developments in
high street shopping.  First though over to Hilary Tindle for a summary of the
main news in the morning papers.

HOST H.T.:  Both our regional papers today use the high-jacked airliner as their
main international front page story.  In the region, they concentrate on the
pollution scare on the River Leman.  Now for more details...

HOST J.D:  Thank you, Hilary.  Now for something a little bit more cheerful.
Have you ever dreamed of scoring six goals in one match?  Local hockey star
Tricia Matthews did precisely that in the local senior league on Saturday.  Tell
me, Tricia, what did it feel like when you scored the last one?

GUEST T.M:   (unscripted)...

HOST J.D.:   (semi-scripting)   What did rest of team think?
Any celebration?
Family reactions?
Tips for young listeners?
Future plans?
```

1 As a Production Team, identify which sections of your proposed programme should be scripted in full and which should be semi-scripted.
2 Write those sections which can be fully scripted.
3 Write down the key words or questions which will guide the semi-scripted sections of the broadcast.

ACTIVITY 9

SKILLS
Assembling a script

RESOURCES
Completed Programme Proposal Form, script sections, paper

Filling out the Script

From your **Programme Proposal Form,** your research and your writing, you have produced the scripts for the *sections* of your programme. Now you need to link the sections together with a script for the Host or Presenter. Most of this linking material can be fully scripted but it might also include semi-scripted and unscripted material.

To keep listeners interested and wanting to stay tuned the Presenter must:

- Comment on what has just been heard.
- Introduce new items.
- Tempt the listener with what is to happen later in the programme.
- Build up the atmosphere – sound cheerful or sad, tell a joke at the right moment.
- Introduce people in a way which will make them feel at ease.

1. As a team, try out all the sections to make sure they sound natural. Re-write where necessary.
2. Now write and try out the link script for the Host or Presenter.
3. Rehearse the full programme.

RADIO WIDEAWAKE

ACTIVITY 10

Sounds good!

SKILLS
Team work, using scripts, recording speech

RESOURCES
Scripts, recording equipment, quiet area for recording

☐ You have written the script for your programme and adjusted it so that it will fit the agreed time limit. Now it is time to make the demonstration tape of your programme.

This will require good organisation, so that everyone in your Production Team knows exactly what to do and when to do it. You cannot afford to make a mess of things during a recording session.

1. Agree who is to play what role during the recording and how the studio is to be arranged. (You will find essential advice on SETTING UP THE STUDIO in SKILLS KIT 9 on page 109.)
2. Try recording a small part of your programme first of all. Listen to the results. Make necessary adjustments to the script, the studio and instructions to personnel.
3. Record your whole programme when the recording studio is free.
4. While you are waiting or after you have made your recording, see the next item.

GOOD LUCK!

ACTIVITY 11 — Meanwhile . . .

SKILLS
Informative writing

RESOURCES
Radio Times and *TV Times*, paper

☐ No radio station has a separate recording studio for each programme broadcast, so there has to be a booking system. Production teams must plan their work so that they can make good use of the time while they are waiting for their turn in the studio. Whilst you are waiting, here are some jobs for you to do.

"Radio Times" entry

In your local paper, radio programmes are often just listed by their name alongside the time of the broadcast. In the *Radio Times* radio pages, though, there is a lot more space for information about each programme.

1 Look carefully at the way your kind of programme is described in a recent copy of the *Radio Times*.
2 As a team write a similar short passage to describe your programme. Make sure it is clear, informative and attractive. This should be displayed in the classroom to advertise what your programme is going to be about.

Feature for "Wideawake" – the Radio Station Magazine

Some local radio stations publish magazines which give lively background information on people and programmes. You will find similar features in the *Radio Times* and *TV Times*, if your local radio station does not publish its own magazine.
These features are based on popular programmes. They describe what the programmes are about, the people who appear in them, and give background information on the production and so on. An article could include:

- drawings or photographs
- quotations from the programme
- what the production team say about it
- "behind the scenes" chat
- competitions linked to the programmes.

3 Write an article about your programme which can be included in the station's magazine.

RADIO WIDEAWAKE

ACTIVITY 12

The send off

SKILLS
Letter writing

RESOURCES
Paper

☐ When you have finished your recording you must compose a letter to go with your tape to the Station Manager of Radio Wideawake. This is an important letter so you need to think about TAP:
- Topic
- Audience
- Purpose.

(You will find further advice on this in WRITING LETTERS, SKILLS KIT 2 on page 98.)

1. In your group, sort out the information that will explain your demonstration when you send it to the radio station.
2. Each person in the group should draft a letter which contains this information. Remember that you are sending it to:

> The Station Manager,
> Radio Wideawake,
> William Cotton House,
> 715 Tempus Road,
> Upton

3. Read your letters to each other and produce an agreed version to send.

ACTIVITY 13

Going public

SKILLS

Appreciative listening, analysis, discussion

RESOURCES

Demonstration tapes, tape recorders, letters, paper

☐ The time has come to share the results of all your hard work!
Meet as a Selection Panel of Radio Wideawake. Remember what you said you were looking for in the original advertisement:

- programmes which are well produced
- programmes which show initiative
- programmes which show new ideas

1 Arrange to listen to all the tapes and to read the letters that accompany them. This can be done in groups or as a whole class.

2 Each Production Team should be allowed a few minutes to introduce its tape and explain what it set out to do.

3 The Selection Panel sets out to encourage talent. It is not interested in flaws or weaknesses. Listen for good points in each programme. Discuss and make a list of these.

4 After listening to a tape and listing its good points, discuss these with the Production Team.

ACTIVITY 14

Golden Mike Awards

SKILLS

Appreciative listening, preparing a formal talk

RESOURCES

Demonstration tapes, recorders, awards

☐ Radio Wideawake proposes to present Golden Mike Awards for the best demonstration tape it has received.

All branches of the entertainment industry present awards each year. Certain programmes and programme makers are nominated for an award in different categories; for example, best journalist, best light entertainment, best factual programme and so on. People vote in a secret ballot and the results are revealed by opening sealed envelopes at a special ceremony.

At the ceremony excerpts from some of the nominations are played. The Host describes the best features of each programme or person nominated. This builds up the tension until finally the envelopes are opened and the names of the winners are revealed.

Presentations are made – perhaps a scroll with a commendation on it or a specially designed cup or some other trophy. The winners make brief speeches. Everyone has a good time!

1. Decide on categories for the awards.
2. Make items to be presented as the awards – scrolls, cups, etc.
3. Select the nominations for each award.
4. Hold a ballot so that only one person knows the results. They are put in sealed envelopes.
5. Where appropriate, select an extract from each programme.
6. Write a script for the Host, briefly praising each nomination.
7. Arrange the Awards Ceremony as a formal but enjoyable event.

ACTIVITY 15

And finally . . .

SKILLS

Informative writing, reviewing, displaying materials

RESOURCES

tapes, tape recorders, display areas

☐ There are many ways in which you can continue this project. You may have your own ideas. Here are some to think about.

Script Display

Scripts are often interesting for others to see. When you have finished your programme the scripts may have become dog-eared and scruffy, but other people such as other classes, parents, teachers might be interested in your work.

Throughout this unit you have been producing other written work which could also be of interest to others. Collect all your writing together. Select from it, tidy it up where necessary, and mount it as a wall display. You might need to add explanatory notes or labels to explain what the parts are about.

Listeners' letters

Read listeners' letters in the *Radio Times* and the *TV Times* and produce similar letters about some of the demonstration tapes.

Programme reviews

Some newspapers have a page with reviews of radio programmes. Read one of these to get an idea of its style. Usually reviewers briefly describe the programme's content and give their opinion of it. Try writing a positive review of some of the programmes you have heard.

What next?

Design a completely new programme for your age range and write a proposal to Radio Wideawake.

Tape display

You may want other people to listen to the tapes you have made for Radio Wideawake. If you want to do this, make copies of your tapes so that you have spares in case of loss or damage. Some of the audiences you might try to reach are:
- Your own parents or relatives.
- Another class in the school.
- Users of the school library.
- A parents' evening.

SKILLS KIT 1

Making notes

Before you write anything it is often useful to make notes to clarify your ideas. Here are some suggestions. You may like to work through them with a friend, discussing each step together.

Making notes for planning

1 Think of all the things that are relevant to your TOPIC. Jot these down on rough paper as they occur to you. Let us say you are working on the topic of *Tropical Exploration at Sea*. Your purpose in writing is to produce an article for your class newsheet.

Your collection of ideas might look like this:

| weather | islands | boats |
| people | food | storms |

| explorers | dangers |
| sailors | Pacific Ocean |

2 Decide which of these things are the MAIN ideas you want to work on. Under each MAIN idea, list further ideas which relate to it. You could cluster these in a web diagram like this one for the main idea of WEATHER.

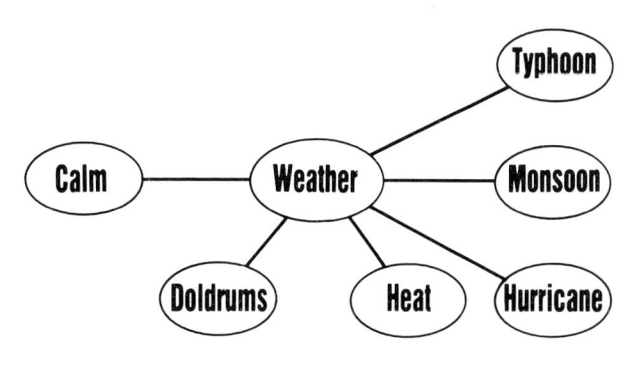

```
        Typhoon
         /
Calm — Weather — Monsoon
       / | \
  Doldrums Heat Hurricane
```

3 Develop each of your MAIN ideas in this way. This will help you to see what further information you need to find out.
4 Now put your MAIN ideas into an order that suits your purpose.
5 Sometimes these rough notes will be enough for what you want to do. From them you can go on to write about your topic. Sometimes you will need to read further to write about your topic. If you are likely to need to return to your notes, write them out neatly, so you can make sense of them later.

Making notes from books

Read Skills Kit 7 on READING FOR INFORMATION before you read this section.

1 When you are making notes from a book, write as little as possible. *Never* copy great chunks. If there is something you want to quote word for word, then copy it, note the source (Who wrote it? In what book? When?) and acknowledge this when you use it in your own writing.
2 What should you do instead of copying? For example, how would you make notes from this information?

> The best means of surviving in arctic conditions, if you are caught in a blizzard in a pine tree area, is to burrow under the lower branches of a large tree. Here you will find that the snow has not filtered through the lower branches and there should be a space in which to shelter. You may need to provide an air hole to the surface in order to breathe.

You would jot down, as briefly as possible, the main information. Your notes might be something like this:

Best way to survive arctic blizzard —
1) Find space under large pine.
2) Make air hole in snow.

You have shrunk 72 words to 16.

There is enough information to JOG YOUR MEMORY – and that is what notes are for.

3 Keep your notes brief and simple. Use:
   - 'key' words to help you remember important ideas
   - dashes to separate bits of information
   - numbers when you list things
   - shortened (abbreviated) words which you could write out in full for public writing.

4 Here are some standard abbreviations often used in note taking from written material or a talk.

       & = and
       ∴ = therefore, so
       ∴ = because

Words can be abbreviated by writing only one syllable, so blizz = blizzard, arct = arctic. But be sure you know what your abbreviations mean when you read them later!

5 It is a good idea to write on your notes where you got the information from:
   - the title of the book or article
   - the author's name
   - the publisher of the book or name of the magazine
   - the date of publication.

You can then refer back to your source of information if you need to.

SKILLS KIT 97

SKILLS KIT 2

Writing letters

Before writing

When you write a letter, there are three main points to consider:

1. Topic (T) – what you want to write about – what information you want to pass on.
2. Audience (A) – whom you are writing to – how well you know the person – how formal or informal to be.
3. Purpose (P) – why you are writing – to give information, ask questions, persuade, complain, etc.

Always think about these TAP points. What do you want to say? Who is the letter for? Why are you writing?

If you are writing an *informal* letter to a friend you will not, of course, spend a lot of time thinking about Topic, Audience, Purpose. But even when you are writing to a friend you may want to jot down the main things you plan to write about – then you're sure to include them all.

When you are writing a *formal* letter it is important to go through the TAP points.

Planning

Jot down all the points you want to get across in the letter. Use single words or phrases.

Let us say that you are writing to ask a tourist office for information about travel in the Pacific.

Your list might be:

Why I'm writing. *When to visit?*
Who I am. *How to get there?*
Climate? *Where to stay?*

Now decide which of these are MAIN ideas which can be the basis of a paragraph. What is the best order for your paragraphs? Which ideas are linked to the main ideas?

Drafting

It is often wise to make a draft (rough copy) first. Here are some suggestions about drafting your letter.

- The opening paragraph should say *why* you are writing. For example:

I am writing to ask for information about Tropical Island. I plan to use this information for a project in my school.

- The next paragraph, or paragraphs, should carry the other information you want to give or ask. Help your reader by beginning each paragraph with a *signpost sentence* which explains what that paragraph is going to be about. For example:

I would particularly like information about the number of tourists who visit the island each year.

- The last paragraph usually says what you hope will happen next as a result of your letter. For example:

I look forward to receiving some information about Tropical Island from you. Thank you for your help.

Layout

Formal letters are usually laid out in a special way. Look at the example on the following page to see how and why this is done.

3 Details of the person or people you want to read your letter. The first line gives their name or position. The other lines give the address you are writing to. These details will also appear on the envelope, but envelopes are often thrown away, so it is important that your letter contains this information as well.

1 Your address, to show where the letter has come from and to show where to send a reply. If you have a telephone number, you can add this as the last line of this section.

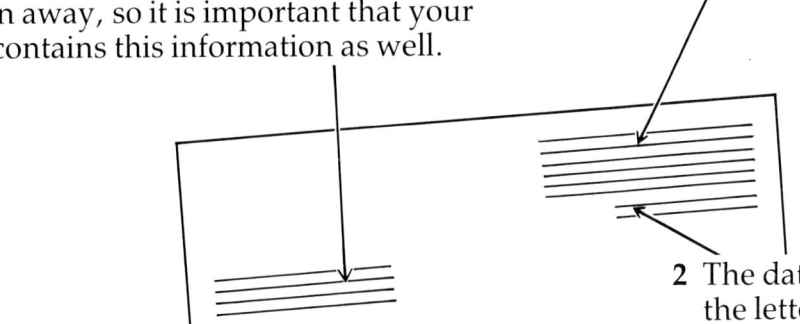

2 The date, to show your reader when the letter was written.

4 This greeting establishes what sort of relationship you are setting up with your reader. It is important to get this right. The greeting depends upon how well you know the person you are writing to:
Dear Peter: to someone you know personally
Dear Mr Jones: to someone you know by name
Dear Sir or Madam: to someone whose name you do not know.

5 Here are the main contents of your letter. The first paragraph should set out briefly what you are writing about and why. It helps your reader to have this information, especially if she or he is a busy person. It also suggests that you are a well-organised and thoughtful person.

The paragraphs in the main section set out what you want to write about.

The final paragraph sums up what you have been writing about and suggests what you might want your reader to do next.

6 This farewell signals the end of the letter and reminds your reader of the sort of relationship you set up with the greeting. The farewell matches the formality of the greeting:
Dear Peter + Yours, Yours sincerely,
Dear Miss Jones + Yours sincerely,
Dear Sir (or Madam) + Yours faithfully,

7 Your signature identifies you as the sender of the letter. It may be repeated in print, if your signature is not very clear! Remember that poor handwriting makes your letter less easy to read and that you are trying to make your letter an easy and attractive meeting between you and your reader.

Writing your fair copy

Check what you have written.
- Is it clear?
- Has it enough information?
- Does it give the impression you want to give?

Check your spelling, punctuation and grammar. If you're not absolutely sure of a spelling, look it up in a dictionary.

When you are satisfied with your draft, write out the letter to send. Try to make no mistakes – corrections spoil the look of a letter.

SKILLS KIT 3

Advertising

There are many forms of advertising, including film, radio, television. This SKILLS KIT looks at very brief forms of advertising in print only.

Identifying brief advertisements

1 Magazine advertisments

Collect some examples of advertisements from magazines for one topic, such as sweets, holidays, cars or clothes. Think about how they:

- a keep the language brief and to the point
- b sometimes use catchy language – slang, rhyme, alliteration, deliberate mis-spelling
- c make the most important material catch your eye by:
  using colour
  playing with unusual layout
  choosing different styles of type-face
  weaving language and illustration
- d use pictures – sketches, line drawings, photographs
- e use maps, charts, diagrams.

Think about how they use these techniques:

- a to make the advertisement more attractive
- b to make the meaning stand out more clearly
- c to break up the print.

Study some of these to see how a cheap and simple form of advertising tries to catch your eye.

There are other forms of advertising. See if you can find any of these other examples.

2 Flyer/Handbill

- a Single sheet of paper printed on one or both sides.
- b Posted direct to likely customers or handed out in the street.
- c Very brief – inexpensive to print.
- d Cheapest handbills do not use colour or illustrations.
- e Have to be striking to look at and use language which attracts attention.

3 Box advertisement

- a Small advertisement which appears in a newspaper or magazine, usually with a thin black line around it.
- b Usually has words only although some include simple picture.
- c Language must be brief and attract attention.
- d Might include address to send to for more information.

4 Brochure/Pamphlet

- a One or more folded sheets of paper containing fuller information than most other advertisements.
- b Room for fuller text.
- c Room for attractive pictures, diagrams, charts and any other print devices advertiser can afford.

Choosing your form of advertisement

1 When you are ready to decide what sort of advertising to use, think about:
   - a what you want to advertise
   - b whom you want to attract
   - c what you want them to know
   - d what mood you want to create

2 Choose the type of advertisment which fits your purpose and decide:
   - a how many words to use.
   - b what style to use – amusing, serious, personal, authoritative.
   - c what typefaces and layout to use – block capitals, italic etc.
   - d what illustrations to use.

SKILLS KIT 4

The interview

If you are the interviewer . . . .

1. Read carefully beforehand –
   - all documents which tell you about the position to be filled and what kind of person you are looking for,
   - all documents about the person you are to interview.

2. Make notes of the important points in both kinds of document.
   - Note the qualities needed for the job.
   - Note which of those qualities the applicant seems to have.

3. Work out the most important questions you want to ask *all* applicants – you can compare their answers later.

4. Try not to ask questions to which you already have answers from their application form. Ask them to:
   - give more information,
   - give opinions on how well they have succeeded in what they have done,
   - give views on problems which you think will show what kind of people they are.

5. Compare notes with other interviewers and arrange:
   - who is to act as a chairperson
   - who is to ask what questions
   - and in what order.

6. When an applicant comes in, the chairperson introduces the interviewers and explains what is to happen. Give clear signals to the applicant about whether to shake hands, where to sit. Make each one feel at ease.

7. The chairperson should give clear signals to other interviewers, such as "I'd just like to ask one last question before my colleague takes over."

8. All interviewers should take brief notes of the applicant's answers, but do not spend all your time writing. It is very important to listen carefully.

9. If an applicant does not give a very full answer to a question, ask an additional question. For example "How did you enjoy that experience?"

10. Keep an eye on the time, and keep within the time you have allowed for each interview.

11. When the interviewers have finished all the questions, ask the applicant if they have anything they would like to ask you or tell you about themselves.

12. The chairperson should thank each applicant and make it clear what is to happen next – whether they will be informed by post or on the same day.

13. When all the interviews are complete, the panel discusses the applicants' qualities compared with the job description and makes a decision. Complete all the details on your interview form.

If you are being interviewed . . .

1. Read carefully beforehand –
   - documents which tell you about what you have applied for
   - your application form (if you have made a copy) so that you know what you said about yourself.

2. Make notes on what you think are your strengths.

3. Make notes on what you think are your weaknesses, and think of how you can defend yourself if criticised.

4 Think what questions you might be asked, and how you might answer to bring out your strengths.

5 Do not take your notes into the interview; have them clearly in your mind.

6 At the interview smile and appear relaxed but be formal and polite when you speak. Sit up straight in the chair and keep your hands and feet still.

7 Be sensitive to each member of the panel. Look directly at the interviewers when you answer their questions, and try to make your answers as full as possible.

8 If you are not sure if you have answered the question fully enough, ask the interviewers, "Does that answer your question?"

9 Do not be afraid to ask questions yourself. You may be asked at the end if you have any questions you want to ask, and you should be prepared for this. It shows you have initiative if you have relevant things to say.

10 At the end of the interview, smile and thank the interviewers, shake hands if they offer, and leave when they show you out.

SKILLS KIT 5

Giving a talk

As with written work it is important first to consider TAP:

- your *topic*
- your *audience*
- the *purpose* of your talk

You must also decide how long your talk will last.

Planning

1 Make a web chart showing what you think are the main points of your topic. Then add any ideas which cluster around these main points. (See Skills Kit 1 for an example.)

2 On your web chart identify the areas about which you are less sure and need to find out more information.
Make a separate list of what you need to find out – and where you might find it. Carry out the research you need to fill in the gaps. (See Skills Kit 7 on Reading for information.)

3 On your web chart, add the new information you have found; first the main ideas and then the supporting ones. Next, sort out the order in which you want to talk about your ideas and number them on the chart.

4 At this stage you might find it useful to let a partner look at your notes and comment on them, to help you make your talk clearer.

5 Before you give your talk, write out the main ideas on a sheet of paper or a card.

   a At the top write your title.
   b Below it, write one or two words to help you remember the start of your talk.
   c Use large print to write the main headings of your talk – with two or three lines of space between each heading, or use a new card for each idea.
   d Underneath each main heading write very brief notes about that topic – just enough to help you remember what you want to say.

Rehearsing

Rehearse what you are going to say in private or with a partner. Don't try to learn your talk. Instead, get to know the ideas so well that you can speak easily and naturally, with your notes to help you.

Speaking

1 Before you speak, take a few deep breaths. Deep breathing helps you to relax.

2 Stand comfortably and hold your notes so that you can glance at them. Don't hide behind them! Look at your notes occasionally to make sure that you know where you are in your talk. If you forget a point, you need to know where to find it.

3 Talk to your audience naturally, slowly and clearly.

4 Look at your audience. Choose a few friendly faces among them and make sure that you look around the room at them as you speak. In this way you seem to be talking to the whole class as individuals.

6 If your audience looks puzzled, you may have to explain things more fully. You may be able to invite questions at the end.

7 Always try to sound as if you are interested in your subject and want to share it with your audience. Vary your pace, making important points more slowly than less important ones. Try to vary how loud or low you speak – but always make sure those at the back can hear every word.

SKILLS KIT 6

Designing a questionnaire

A questionnaire is a list of questions. In a survey it can be used in two ways.

1. You can give it to people and ask them to write their answers on it and give it back to you later.
2. You can use it to interview people to make sure that you ask everyone the same questions.

Planning a questionnaire

1. Discuss with others the purpose of your survey and all the information you want to find out from it. Don't be afraid to jot down everything that comes into your mind. Make a list or web chart as you go (See Skills Kit 1 for an example.)

2. Go over your chart or list and cluster ideas together. Then choose everything which is essential. You might underline or circle these points in a bright colour. Then ignore everything else. You now know what you want to find out. The next job is to turn these points into questions.

3. The success of a questionnaire depends on the sorts of questions you ask. Think carefully about the sorts of questions which will help you to obtain the information you want. There are different kinds of questions you can use.

- CLOSED QUESTIONS e.g. *How many times a week do you shop here?*
  This question will give you a definite answer which you can later use in a graph.

  Another sort of closed question will result in a *yes/no* answer. Be careful though! If you ask "Do you shop here very often?" one person might think twice a week was very often and say "Yes". Another might think it was not often and say "No." You can get round this by asking "Do you shop here daily/once or twice a week/less often?"

- OPINION QUESTIONS e.g. *Some people think this pavement is too narrow for mothers with prams. What do you think?*
  Three kinds of answer are possible with opinion questions
  agree/neither agree nor disagree/disagree
  The response to an opinion question can be ticked in a box on the form.
  Be careful to keep your questions neutral. If you ask this question as "The pavement is too narrow for mothers with prams. Do you agree?" you are likely to sway the answer.

- OPEN QUESTIONS, e.g. *Why do you shop here?*

  Open questions allow people to say as much as they like in any way that they like. You can obtain a lot of information by using open questions but it may be difficult to write it all down and sift out what you want to know.

4. It is likely that you will use all three kinds of question, depending on what information you are seeking and the detail you need. CLOSED and OPINION questions are easy to handle but OPEN questions may give you a lot more interesting information.

5. If you use the questionnaire for interviewing you will have to decide on how to record the answers. OPEN questions need a lot of space under each of them for the answers.

6. You might need certain details about the people responding to your questionnaire. For instance you might want to interview old people or teenagers or shop-keepers to get their

different points of view. Later, you might want to group their answers together so note which of your groups a person belongs to: 'Pensioner,' 'teenager,' 'shopkeeper'. Be sensitive though. Many people do not like to be asked personal questions – about their age for instance. Decide what you need to know about the people replying and design a space for this information at the top of your questionnaire. People who respond to questionnaires are never named.

7 Good questionnaire design should make it easy for the person responding to help you and should make it easy for you to handle the information afterwards. Try your questionnaire out on a couple of people first of all to make sure that it works and adjust it if necessary.

8 Be polite at all times. Explain who you are, why you are seeking information and what will happen to the results. Assure people that they will remain anonymous. If anybody is uneasy about answering the questionnaire, let them go.

9 You need a new copy of the questionnaire form for each person who provides you with information.

SKILLS KIT 7

Reading for Information

For this skill your *purpose* is to find particular pieces of information which you need about a topic you are studying. You do not always need to read a book from cover to cover to find the information you are looking for.

Skimming for information

When you find a book which looks as if it contains information you need, have a quick look through it before you start reading.

Look at:
- a The *title* on the cover, spine or title page;
- b The back or flaps of a paper cover to see if there is a description of the book;
- c the illustrations;
- d the first few pages
- e the last few pages.

Now, if you think the book looks useful, look further.

Noting Useful Chapters and Pages

Let us suppose your *purpose* is to find material on survival in the tropics. You have found a copy of Anthony Greenbank's *Survival for Young People*. You have looked through it quickly. It looks promising. But you may not need to read all 158 pages for your present purpose. What should you do?

- a Turn to the *Contents* list. It's at the front of the book, usually after the title page. Are any of the chapters on tropical survival? This book looks promising. Chapter 5 is called *Survival journey on land*. That may be useful. But chapter 4, *Keeping warm in a catastrophe*, will not. You've already saved yourself having to read the 18 pages of Chapter 4!
- b Make a note of the title and the page number of any other chapters that interest you. Leave a few lines between each for your notes.
- c Turn to the *Index* at the back of the book. See which items fit your topic.

For instance, if you want to find out about food, these look promising:

Birds, eggs page 129
Cooking, survival, pages 136–141
Fish, catching, page 130

Note these page references in the space left under your chosen chapter titles. You now know which pages you want to look at first. You know the chapters you will read more carefully if you have time.

Reading and taking notes

How should your read to take notes? Let's assume that you want to read a chapter. A good writer helps you:

- a by explaining what the chapter is going to be about in the first one or two paragraphs;
- b by explaining what each paragraph is going to be about in its first one or two sentences.
- c by summing up what the chapter has been about in its last two or three paragraphs.

Skim through the chapter

- a Read the first couple of paragraphs.
- b Read the first sentence or two of each paragraph.
- c Reading the last couple of paragraphs.

You will be surprised by how much you have learned!

You have skimmed the chapter and have a rough idea what it is about.
Now go back to the parts of the chapter which looked interesting and
read them more slowly to make your notes. (This system often works
on newspaper and magazine articles as well.)

See SKILLS KIT 1 on MAKING NOTES for help on how to record your information.

SKILLS KIT 8

The Broadcaster's training manual

Part I: Planning a programme

Designing a programme

1 Length

Any programme or item in a programme is given a time slot to fill to the nearest second. Concentrate on quality rather than length. A lively *two or three minute* item is better than twenty minutes of badly written material presented at a slow pace.

Time your material as you script it – read it out and make a note of how long parts are in minutes and seconds. Then you can cut the material to fit the exact programme length more easily.

2 Sections

If your material is a complete programme, divide the time into sections. Aim for variety by contrasting the *content* of the sections. For instance if you have two sections on fashion in a magazine programme, place something different such as a sports item between them.

Contrast how you *present* the sections so that there is a balance between:

- interview and commentary
- one voice and several voices
- different kinds of voice and accent
- music, talk and other kinds of sound
- different kinds of music

3 Programme links

Sections within a programme are often linked by a *Host* who tells listeners what is going to happen next, and gives "trailers" of what will happen later in the programme. Sections can be introduced by different *Presenters* including the Host.

4 Opening a programme

Programmes often start with a Continuity Announcer saying

- what the programme is called
- who the Host is
- what the show has in it today

It is a good idea to script this so that the Continuity Announcer says exactly what is intended briefly and clearly.

Then the "Host" of the programme takes over to welcome the listeners.

Many programmes use signature or theme tunes, so that people can recognise them. See if you can find the right piece of music to start and end your programme.

5 Closing a programme

A Host rounds off the programme in the final minute by summarising what has gone on and perhaps saying what will be in the next one. Either the Host reads the programme credits (see the Programme Credits Form) or the Continuity Announcer who follows reads them.

Remember that the programme *must* end to the nearest second of the agreed time. Use a watch which shows seconds clearly when you rehearse your material and note down times on the script frequently. During the broadcast, one of the Production Staff should watch the time carefully and signal silently to the Presenters how the time is going.

6 Slots

In the breaks between programmes or sections in a programme there can be a variety of material – news and weather announcements, as well as traffic information and emergency public information "flashes".

In a commercial radio station, there will be at least one slot in every programme for advertisements. Advertisements, including jingles and background music, are usually created by a separate department, but each group can be responsible for its own. You can invent your own products to advertise or use familiar products known to you.

Each of these 'slots' must be timed to fit into the complete programme.

SKILLS KIT 9

The Broadcaster's training manual

Part II: Recording a programme

Setting up the studio

1 Where to record

A room which does not echo is best. Carpets, curtains and soft materials help to stop echo, so a cloak room or backstage behind heavy curtains or a bookstore cupboard are all possible areas. If you cannot find such a room, place sound-deadening material such as coats under and behind the microphone.

Your studio should be away from other distracting noises – people walking, talking, telephones ringing. Alternatively, record during a quiet time of the day. Beware of school bells ringing during a recording!

Make sure in designing the studio layout that:
- performers can move easily towards and away from the microphone
- the microphone is not knocked or touched by people moving about.

2 The Recorder

A simple cassette recorder will do. It is important to know its controls well. Try to use one with a counter so that you can find the exact place if you need to re-record part of a programme.

It is very difficult to edit a cassette tape, so scripts must be recorded in the right order. A *pause button* will allow you to start and stop the recording without making clicks on the tape. Use it to build up a good recording, section by section. If you note the number on the counter each time, you can return accurately to the right place.

If your sound recording level is not automatic you will be able to use the *volume control* to "fade" up (become louder) or down (become quieter). That can be used in drama to indicate a scene change or the passing of time.

3 The microphone

A separate microphone is best. Some built-in microphones pick up the hum of the tape-recorder's motor, and the people speaking have to stand very close to the machine. Place the microphone on a stand or cushioned surface.

Microphones pick up taps, bangs, squeaks and rattles louder than they sound in real life. Make sure that performers move around as little as possible; that everyone tiptoes about; that no one makes a chair creak, or knocks a table, particularly if the microphone is on it. Scripts make a rustling noise that microphones exaggerate. Warn everyone to turn pages very gently, or to float them to the floor when they have been read.

4 Where speakers stand

Experiment to find the best place for the recorder and other equipment so that people are not tripping up over wires and so that technicians can operate equipment out of the way of performers.

Speak towards the microphone, and not up at the ceiling. There is no need to look at each other; facing the microphone is the important thing. Test what is the most effective distance from the microphone for the performers. Usually the nearer the speaker is, the clearer the sound, but when several people speak in a discussion/ advertisement/interview, they need to be in a semi-circle around the microphone.

If sound effects are to be performed live, you will need space for the operators as well in the recording area.

5 Other sound sources

Production teams may want to introduce *pre-recorded sound*, such as music, interviews or sound effects. A cassette player is better than a record player for this because you can set up the tape at the right point more exactly. You might find it useful to have more than one tape recorder if you are introducing more than one item of pre-recorded material.

6 Studio Management

During recording, technicians and performers cannot talk to each other about how things are going, or ask if the recorder is on or off. You need a system of completely silent *sign language*.
A technician should act as Studio Manager for a recording session. That means that she or he is in charge of the recording and:

- counts down ("5, 4, 3, 2, 1") to the beginning of the recording
- cues the first speaker with a gesture to start speaking when the tape is running
- cues all other speakers and any pre-recorded material as called for in the script
- checks that no unwanted noise is being made
- decides to re-record any section of a programme if necessary.

7 Rehearsal

You cannot know what the best studio layout, microphone distance and recording level setting will be without experimenting and rehearsing all the time that scripting is going on. If a Production Team is being too ambitious, they can see what is not possible before they go too far the wrong way.

Radio programmes are a performance in front of an unseen audience. Like any performance, rehearsal improves the result. As you write the script, read it aloud, line by line to see if it sounds natural and interesting. As you finish sections, read them to your team for comment. When you have all your material written, practise the programme until it sounds smooth and confident.

Some of the material may be only semi-scripted, for example in an interview. In that case, try out the scripted parts, such as questions, on team members to see if they work. If anyone says "What are you getting at?" you will need to change the question.

If you have Guests on the programme, talk with them about what you would like to ask them, and let them tell you what they want to say. Make sure you all agree – that is the only rehearsal you can have. Then write guidelines for the interviewer using what has been agreed. If the Guests are to sound natural they should talk without a script.